The Relevance of the Leadership Standards: A New Order of Business for Principals

The Relevance of the Leadership Standards: A New Order of Business for Principals

Leslie Jones

ROWMAN & LITTLEFIELD
Lanham • Boulder • New York • London

Published by Rowman & Littlefield
A wholly owned subsidiary of The Rowman & Littlefield Publishing Group, Inc.
4501 Forbes Boulevard, Suite 200, Lanham, Maryland 20706
www.rowman.com

Unit A, Whitacre Mews, 26–34 Stannary Street, London SE11 4AB

Copyright © 2017 by Leslie Jones

All rights reserved. No part of this book may be reproduced in any form or by any electronic or mechanical means, including information storage and retrieval systems, without written permission from the publisher, except by a reviewer who may quote passages in a review.

British Library Cataloguing in Publication Information Available

Library of Congress Cataloging-in-Publication Data
ISBN 978-1-4758-3378-2 (cloth : alk. paper)
ISBN 978-1-4758-3379-9 (pbk. : alk. paper)
ISBN 978-1-4758-3380-5 (electronic)

∞™ The paper used in this publication meets the minimum requirements of American National Standard for Information Sciences—Permanence of Paper for Printed Library Materials, ANSI/NISO Z39.48–1992.

Printed in the United States of America

*In Memory of My Mother
Marion Landry Jones*

Contents

Foreword ix

Preface xi

Acknowledgments xiii

1 Introduction, an Overview of the Processes for the Development of ISLLC to PSEL 1
 Introduction 1
 Evolution of Standards 1
 Educational Leadership Constituent Council (ELCC) 3
 NELP 6
 PSEL 7
 Standard 1: Mission, Vision, and Core Values 8
 Standard 2: Ethics and Professional Norms 9
 Standard 3: Equity and Cultural Responsiveness 9
 Standard 4: Curriculum, Instruction, and Assessment 10
 Standard 5: Community of Care and Support for Students 11
 Standard 6: Professional Capacity of School Personnel 12
 Standard 7: Professional Community for Teachers and Staff 12
 Standard 8: Meaningful Engagement of Families and Community 13
 Standard 9: Operations and Management 14
 Standard 10: School Improvement 15
 PSEL Changes 16

2	Professional Standards for Educational Leaders: Standards 1, 2, 3, and 10: "The Drivers" Standard 2: Ethics and Professional Norms 28 Case 1: Preparing for a New Leadership Role 33	21
3	Professional Standards for Educational Leaders: Standards 4 and 5: "The Core" Standard 5 of PSEL Has a Focus on Teaching and Learning 45	37
4	Professional Standards for Educational Leaders: Standards 6, 7, 8, and 9: The "Supports" Standard 7: Professional Community for Teachers and Staff 61 Standard 8: Meaningful Engagement of Families and Community 67 Standard 9: Operations and Management 73	53
5	Where Do We Go from Here?	85
	About the Author	95

Foreword

The development of the Interstate School Leaders Licensure Consortium (ISLLC) Standards, now the Professional Standards for Educational Leaders (PSEL), has served as a catalyst to propel the profession toward an improved state of practice. Subsequently, the development of the Educational Leadership Constituent Council (ELCC) Standards, now the National Educational Leadership Preparation (NELP) Standards, has assisted preparation programs in designing experiences that guide those preparing for educational leadership toward the realities that challenge their preparation and readiness to lead.

Since 1996, when the initial ISLLC Standards were released through the most current version of the PSEL (2015), these standards have undergone revisions in order to meet the changing demands faced by the profession. PSEL contain significant changes to the former ISLLC Standards, 2008, These changes, both in number and in content, reflect an increased emphasis on student learning and achievement. As with previous standards, in a few years it will be necessary to revise these standards to meet changing realities of the profession.

The program standards, ELCC, now NELP, are predicated on the leader standards, and these new standards are significantly impacting the design of leader preparation programs. As colleges and universities adapt their program delivery to the new standards, there is guidance required to assist this process. *School and District Leaders for 2020* is a wonderful resource for program development. This text unpacks the standards as well as provides a detailed comparison of the ISLLC 2008 and ELCC 2011 to the current standards.

For students in preparation programs, understanding the PSEL and NELP Standards is necessary to fully take advantage of preparing for professional practice. This text is a valuable tool for programs and students. Understanding the intricacies of the standards provides a metric for measuring the quality of your preparation and assessing the degree of your readiness to meet the demands of the job.

School and District Leaders for 2020 provides readers with an in-depth examination of both the PSEL and NELP Standards. A comparison of the previous ISLLC and ELCC Standards is another valuable tool for building and participating in a quality preparation program. The author has provided valuable links to other resources and documents that assist the reader's development of an understanding of the standards and the role these standards play in articulating the demands and expectations of the profession.

The reality for those designing and delivering preparation programs and those preparing to enter the profession the level of accountability continues to increase as changes in demographics, international comparison, and globalization impact the level of practice expected by school leaders. This book is an excellent tool for assisting in meeting the realities brought on by these factors.

Richard A. Flanary
Co-chair of the 2008 ISLLC Standards Revision
Former Deputy Executive Director for Programs
& Services, NASSP
Leadership Development Consultant

Preface

The work of school leaders is critical in this era, and there is heightened attention on the roles of the leaders as linked to student achievement and school improvement; school culture and climate; and the variables that impact achievement, improvement, culture, and climate. The demands on school leaders have significantly changed. About a decade ago, the Southern Educational Regional Board suggested that school leaders impact as much as 20 percent of the achievement in schools. A few years later, the potential impact of school leaders increased to 25 percent. Throughout the chapters, the reoccurring concepts regarding the work of leaders are discussed.

There is need for leaders to move student learning and to respond to changes in education and challenges, which are contributing factors to the development of the Professional Standards for Educational Leaders (PSEL). In chapter 1 and in other chapters of the book, the links and importance between educational leadership and student learning are provided. The standards provide a framework of the knowledge and skills needed for school leaders to be prepared for the challenges.

PSEL are professional standards for school leaders that apply to assistant principals and principals with concepts applicable to district-level leadership. PSEL are presented as the replacement standards for the Interstate School Leaders Licensure Consortium Standards. The National Educational Leadership Preparation (NELP) Standards are presented as the replacement standards for the Educational Leadership Constituent Council. Five chapters are included in the publication with a description of what is needed for school leaders from a standards-based approach. The objectives for publication include the following:

- Reviewing the history of the Interstate School Leaders Licensure Consortium (ISLLC) Standards—revised to the PSEL and the importance of standards for leaders;
- Discussing the shift in the PSEL to a focus on "students";
- Discussing the practicalities of PSEL for school leaders.

The publication is a guide to assist school leaders in applying the principles of the standards to daily practices. It will become more and more critical for leaders to support teachers in responding to the needs of diverse populations. As early as 1991, Graham noted that we can no longer afford to "slip" students through weak curriculum. This is a tool to help strengthen curriculum and other aspects that fall within the responsibility of school leaders.

Acknowledgments

I acknowledge God for His sovereignty as God and for keeping my soul. I am grateful for the royal inheritance as a believer. I have been supported by many family members, colleagues, and a very dedicated graduate student: Victoria Rodriguez. My parents Dr. Lloyd Jones and the late Marion Jones provide constant love and support; my siblings—Lloyd III (Patsy), Lenette (Buddy), and Lorann (James)—are dedicated to many of my causes; and my nieces and nephews are inspirational—Meagan, Desmond, Jasmine, Daniel, Maya, Jannah, and James. I am grateful for Johnny Hamilton and his unwavering support. I dedicate this volume to the memory of my mother: Marion Jones.

Chapter 1

Introduction, an Overview of the Processes for the Development of ISLLC to PSEL

INTRODUCTION

In this chapter, an overview of the processes for the development of the Interstate School Leaders Licensure Consortium (ISLLC) Standards and Professional Standards for Educational Leaders (PSEL) is included. To ensure that candidates were and are prepared to meet the demands of leadership, the Council of Chief State School Officers (CCSSO) has been an active voice for developing leadership standards since 1996.

The first ISLLC Standards were adopted in 1998. A collaborative effort between CCSSO and National Policy Board for Educational Administration (NPBEA) led to the adoption of the 2015 PSEL. The 2015 standards include four additional standards. There are several further differences; however, one of the differences is that there is a more intense focus on student achievement.

EVOLUTION OF STANDARDS

The first set of leadership standards for educational leaders was published in 1996 by CCSSO. Modest revisions were published in 2008 to the ISLLC Standards based on pertinent research in 2008. ISLLC is in transition to the PSEL (2015). However, it is suggested that the ISLLC Standards put in place were a good starting point of principles, dispositions, and skills for effective leaders.[1]

Over the years, other entities have developed standards for leaders. The Educational Leadership Constituent Council (ELCC) parallels ISLLC;

both sets of standards have been embraced by most membership entities included in PSEL (American Association of Colleges of Teacher Education, American Association of School Administrators, Council for the Accreditation of Educator Preparation, Council of Chief State School Officers, National Association of Elementary School Principals, National Council of Professors of Educational Administration, National School Boards Association, and the University Council for Educational Administration).

The major difference in ISLLC and ELCC is the nature of the standards. ELCC was designed specifically for programs of educational leadership with the purpose of program development and alignment of programs. ISLLC was designed for practitioners. ISLLC has been phased out with the phasing in of the PSEL 2015. ELCC is phasing out with the proposed adoption of the National Educational Leadership Preparation Standards (NELP). The focus of NELP is for program development and alignment, and the focus of PSEL is on practicalities.

Anthes[2] found that all educational leadership standards generally align to the following categories:

- Developing and articulating a vision;
- Strategic decision making and implementation;
- Promoting community engagement;
- Creating a culture of learning;
- Using data appropriately;
- Understanding curriculum and instruction;
- Seeking engagement from all staff;
- Understanding effective management;
- Providing high-quality professional growth opportunities to staff; and
- Communicating effectively and honestly with staff, students, and community members.

According to the article *About ISLLC*[3] the ISLLC Standards are based on:

- A thorough analysis of what is known about effective educational leadership at the school levels;
- A comprehensive examination of the best thinking about the types of leadership that will be for tomorrow's schools;
- Syntheses of the thoughtful work on administrator standards developed by various national organizations, professional associations, and reform commissions; and
- In-depth discussions of leadership and administrative standards by leaders within each of those involved in the ISLLC.

Each of the standards begins with the same phrase: "A school administrator is an educational leader who promotes the success of all students by." The following is the remaining text of the standards:

- Standard 1 (The Vision of Learning) facilitating the development, articulation, implementation, and stewardship of a vision of learning that is shared and supported by the school community;
- Standard 2 (The Culture of Teaching and Learning) advocating, nurturing, and sustaining a school culture and instructional program conducive to student learning and staff professional growth;
- Standard 3 (Management of Learning) ensuring management of the organization, operations, and resources for a safe, efficient, and effective learning environment;
- Standard 4 (Relations with Broader Community to Foster Learning) collaborating with families and community members, responding to diverse community interests, and needs, and mobilizing community resources;
- Standard 5 (Integrity, Fairness, and Ethics in Learning) acting with integrity, with fairness, and in an ethical manner; and
- Standard 6 (The Political, Social, Economic, Legal, and Cultural Context of Learning) understanding, responding to, and influencing the larger political, social, economic, legal, and cultural context.

EDUCATIONAL LEADERSHIP CONSTITUENT COUNCIL (ELCC)

The ELCC Standards are an extension of the ISLLC Standards. The American Association for School Administrators (AASA), the American Association for Supervision and Curriculum Development (ASCD), the National Association of Secondary School Principals (NASSP), and the National Association for Elementary School Principals (NAESP) developed the ELCC Standards from ISLLC adding one standard on the basis of a year-long internship.

The following are the ELCC Standards:

- Standard 1. A school district leader is an educational leader who has the knowledge and ability to promote the success of all students by facilitating the development, articulation, implementation, and stewardship of a school or district vision of learning that is supported by the school community;
- Standard 2. A school district leader is an educational leader who has the knowledge and ability to promote the success of all students by promoting a positive school culture, providing an effective instructional program,

applying best practices to student learning, and designing comprehensive professional growth plans for staff;
- Standard 3. A school district leader is an educational leader who has the knowledge and ability to promote the success of all students by managing the organization, operations, and resources in a way that promotes a safe, efficient, and effective learning environment;
- Standard 4. A school district leader is an educational leader who has the knowledge and ability to promote the success of all students by collaborating with families and other community members, responding to diverse community interests and needs, and mobilizing community resources;
- Standard 5. A school district leader is an educational leader who has the knowledge and ability to promote the success of all students by acting with integrity and fairness and in an ethical manner;
- Standard 6. A school district leader is an educational leader who has the knowledge and ability to promote the success of all students by understanding, responding to, and influencing the larger political, social, economic, legal, and cultural context; and
- Standard 7. The internship provides significant opportunities for candidates to synthesize and apply the knowledge and practice and develop the skills identified in Standards 1–6 through substantial, sustained, standards-based work in real settings, planned and guided cooperatively by the institution and school district personnel for graduate credit.

In table 1.1, an abbreviated chart of the ISLLC (2008) and ELCC (2011) Standards is included. In the chart, the alignment between and across standards

Table 1.1. Abbreviated Chart of ISLLC (2008) and ELCC (2011) Alignment

ISLLC 2008	ELCC 2011
Standard 1: A school administrator is an educational leader who promotes the success of all students by facilitating the development, articulation, implementation, and stewardship of a vision of learning that is shared and supported by the school community (Visionary Leadership)	Standard 1: Candidates who complete the program are educational leaders who have the knowledge and ability to promote the success of all students by facilitating the development, articulation, implementation, and stewardship of a school or district vision of learning supported by the school community.
Standard 2: School administrator is an educational leader who promotes the success of all students by advocating, nurturing, and sustaining a school culture and instructional program conducive to student learning and staff professional development. (Instructional Leadership)	Standard 2: Candidates who complete the program are educational leaders who have the knowledge and ability to promote the success of all students by promoting a positive school culture, providing an effective instructional program, applying best practice to student learning, and designing comprehensive professional growth plans for staff.

ISLLC 2008	ELCC 2011
Standard 3: A school administrator is an educational leader who promotes the success of all students by ensuring management of the organization, operations, and resources for a safe, efficient, and effective learning environment. (Organizational Leadership)	Standard 3: Candidates who complete the program are educational leaders who have the knowledge and ability to promote the success of all students by managing the organization, operations, and resources in a way that promotes a safe, efficient, and effective learning environment.
Standard 4: A school administrator is an educational leader who promotes the success of all students by collaborating with families and community members, responding to diverse community interests and needs, and mobilizing community resources. (Collaborative Leadership)	Standard 4: Candidates who complete the program are educational leaders who have the knowledge and ability to promote the success of all students by collaborating with families and other community members, responding to diverse community interests and needs, and mobilizing community resources.
Standard 5: A school administrator is an educational leader who promotes the success of all students by acting with integrity, fairness, and in an ethical manner. (Ethical Leadership)	Standard 5: Candidates who complete the program are educational leaders who have the knowledge and ability to promote the success of all students by acting with integrity, fairly, and in an ethical manner.
Standard 6: A school administrator is an educational leader who promotes the success of all students by understanding, responding to, and influencing the larger political, social, economic, legal, and cultural context. (Political Leadership)	Standard 6: Candidates who complete the program are educational leaders who have the knowledge and ability to promote the success of all students by understanding, responding to, and influencing the larger political, social, economic, legal, and cultural context.
	Additional ELCC standard not associated with any ISLLC standard **ELCC Standard 7: Internship. The internship provides significant opportunities for candidates to synthesize and apply the knowledge and practice and develop the skills identified in Standards 1–6 through substantial, sustained, standards-based work in real settings, planned and guided cooperatively by the institution and school district personnel for graduate credit.**

is obvious. For instance, in ISLLC 2008: Standard 1 vision is addressed. In ELCC 2011: Standard a vision is also addressed. There are commonalities throughout the standards.

As previously mentioned, the NELP Standards are replacing ELCC Standards.

NELP

The following are the NELP Standards.

Standard One: Mission, Vision, and Core Values

Program completers who successfully complete a building-level educational leadership preparation program understand and demonstrate the capability to promote the success and well-being of each student, teacher, and leader by applying the knowledge, skills, and commitments necessary for (1) a shared mission and vision, (2) a set of core values, (3) a support system, and (4) a school improvement process.

Standard Two: Ethics and Professional Norms

Program completers who successfully complete a building-level educational leadership preparation program understand and demonstrate the capability to promote the success and well-being of each student, teacher, and leader by applying the knowledge, skills, and commitments necessary for (1) professional norms, (2) decision making, (3) educational values, and (4) ethical behavior.

Standard Three: Equity and Cultural Leadership

Program completers who successfully complete a building-level educational leadership preparation program understand and demonstrate the capability to promote the success and well-being of each student, teacher, and leader by applying the knowledge, skills, and commitments necessary for (1) equitable protocols, (2) equitable access, (3) responsive practices, and (4) a supportive school community.

Standard Four: Instructional Leadership

Program completers who successfully complete a building-level educational leadership preparation program understand and demonstrate the capability to promote the success and well-being of each student, teacher, and leader by applying the knowledge, skills, and commitments necessary for (1) learning system, (2) instructional practice, (3) assessment system, and (4) learning supports.

Standard Five: Community and External Leadership

Program completers who successfully complete a building-level educational leadership preparation program understand and demonstrate the capability to promote the success and well-being of each student, teacher, and leader by applying the knowledge, skills, and commitments necessary for (1) effective communication, (2) engagement, (3) partnerships, and (4) advocacy.

Standard Six: Operations and Management

Program completers who successfully complete a building-level educational leadership preparation program understand and demonstrate the capability to promote the success and well-being of each student, teacher, and leader by applying the knowledge, skills, and commitments necessary for (1) management and operation, (2) data and resources, (3) communication systems, and (4) legal compliance.

Standard Seven: Human Resource Leadership

Program completers who successfully complete a building-level educational leadership preparation program understand and demonstrate the capability to promote the success and well-being of each student, teacher, and leader by applying the knowledge, skills, and commitments necessary for (1) human resources, (2) professional culture, (3) workplace conditions, and (4) supervision and evaluation.

Standard Eight: Internship and Clinical Practice

Program completers who successfully complete a building-level educational leadership preparation program engage in a substantial and sustained educational leadership internship experience that developed their ability to promote the success and well-being of each student, teacher, and leader through field experiences and clinical practice within a building setting, monitored and evaluated by a qualified, on-site mentor.

PSEL

The NPBEA has several member organizations that participated and endorsed the PSEL 2015. Many of the entities involved in the development of the 1996 and 2008 ISLLC Standards were involved in the development process of PSEL. The two-year development process of PSEL was very "extensive" involving a review of empirical research with surveys and focus groups from practitioners. Multiple work groups and committees, including over one thousand professionals, participated in the development of the standards that are grounded in real-life experiences of educational leaders.

In both the 2008 ISLLC and the 2011 ELCC Standards, the importance of vision, instructional leadership, managerial leadership, school and community relations, and ethics, and the importance of responding to the larger social order for school leadership are included. Concepts from the previously cited list are also included in the 2016 PSEL. However, many of the principles have greater specificity, and there are additional concepts.

One reason for the transition to the 2015 PSEL Standards is due to the changes in the world we operate today. In Table 1.2, a comparison of the PSEL 2015, ISCLL 2008, and ELCC 2011 Standards is presented. The analogy is often made that schools are replicate of society; society has definitely become more complex, and learners are much more diverse. In addition, schools must prepare students for workplaces of the twenty-first century, and there are greater emphases on accountability and student achievement.

All of the PSEL begin with "Effective Leaders." The following are the PSEL with their standard elements form.[4]

STANDARD 1: MISSION, VISION, AND CORE VALUES

> **Effective educational leaders develop, advocate, and enact a shared mission, vision, and core values of high-quality education and academic success and well-being of each student.**

Effective Leaders

a) Develop an educational mission for the school to promote the academic success and well-being of each student.
b) In collaboration with members of the school and the community and using relevant data, develop and promote a vision for the school on the successful learning and development of each child and on instructional and organizational practices that promote such success.
c) Articulate, advocate, and cultivate core values that define the school's culture and stress the imperative of child-centered education; high expectations and student support; equity, inclusiveness, and social justice; openness, caring, and trust; and continuous improvement.
d) Strategically develop, implement, and evaluate actions to achieve the vision for the school.
e) Review the school's mission and vision and adjust them to changing expectations and opportunities for the school, and changing needs and situations of students.

f) Develop shared understanding of and commitment to mission, vision, and core values within the school and the community.
g) Model and pursue the school's mission, vision, and core values in all aspects of leadership.

STANDARD 2: ETHICS AND PROFESSIONAL NORMS

> **Effective educational leaders act ethically and according to professional norms to promote each student's academic success and well-being.**

Effective Leaders

a) Act ethically and professionally in personal conduct, relationships with others, decision-making, stewardship of the school's resources, and all aspects of school leadership.
b) Act according to and promote the professional norms of integrity, fairness, transparency, trust, collaboration, perseverance, learning, and continuous improvement.
c) Place children at the center of education and accept responsibility for each student's academic success and well-being.
d) Safeguard and promote the values of democracy, individual freedom and responsibility, equity, social justice, community, and diversity.
e) Lead with interpersonal and communication skill, social-emotional insight, and understanding of all students' and staff members' backgrounds and cultures.
f) Provide moral direction for the school and promote ethical and professional behavior among faculty and staff.

STANDARD 3: EQUITY AND CULTURAL RESPONSIVENESS

> **Effective educational leaders strive for equity of educational opportunity and culturally responsive practices to promote each student's academic success and well-being.**

Effective Leaders

a) Ensure that each student is treated fairly, respectfully, and with an understanding of each student's culture and context.
b) Recognize, respect, and employ each student's strengths, diversity, and culture as assets for teaching and learning.
c) Ensure that each student has equitable access to effective teachers, learning opportunities, academic and social support, and other resources necessary for success.
d) Develop student policies and address student misconduct in a positive, fair, and unbiased manner.
e) Confront and alter institutional biases of student marginalization, deficit-based schooling, and low expectations associated with race, class, culture and language, gender and sexual orientation, and disability or special status.
f) Promote the preparation of students to live productively in and contribute to the diverse cultural contexts of a global society.
g) Act with cultural competence and responsiveness in their interactions, decision making, and practice.
h) Address matters of equity and cultural responsiveness in all aspects of leadership.

STANDARD 4: CURRICULUM, INSTRUCTION, AND ASSESSMENT

> **Effective educational leaders develop and support intellectually rigorous and coherent system of curriculum, instruction, and assessment to promote each student's academic success and well-being.**

Effective Leaders

a) Implement coherent systems of curriculum, instruction, and assessment that promote the mission, vision, and core values of the school, embody high expectations for student learning, align with academic standards, and are culturally responsive.
b) Align and focus systems of curriculum, instruction, and assessment within and across grade levels to promote student academic success, love of learning, the identities and habits of learners, and healthy sense of self.

c) Promote instructional practice that is consistent with knowledge of child learning and development, effective pedagogy, and the needs of each student.
d) Ensure instructional practice that is intellectually challenging, authentic to student experiences, recognizes student strengths, and is differentiated and personalized.
e) Promote the effective use of technology in the service of teaching and learning.
f) Employ valid assessments that are consistent with knowledge of child learning and development and technical standards of measurement.
g) Use assessment data appropriately and within technical limitations to monitor student progress and improve instruction.

STANDARD 5: COMMUNITY OF CARE AND SUPPORT FOR STUDENTS

> Effective educational leaders cultivate an inclusive, caring, and supportive school community that promotes the academic success and well-being of each student.

Effective Leaders

a) Build and maintain a safe, caring, and healthy school environment that meets that the academic, social, emotional, and physical needs of each student.
b) Create and sustain a school environment in which each student is known, accepted and valued, trusted and respected, cared for, and encouraged to be an active and responsible member of the school community.
c) Provide coherent systems of academic and social supports, services, extra-curricular activities, and accommodations to meet the range of learning needs of each student.
d) Promote adult-student, student-peer, and school-community relationships that value and support academic learning and positive social and emotional development.
e) Cultivate and reinforce student engagement in school and positive student conduct.
f) Infuse the school's learning environment with the cultures and languages of the school's community.

STANDARD 6: PROFESSIONAL CAPACITY OF SCHOOL PERSONNEL

> **Effective educational leaders develop the professional capacity and practice of school personnel to promote each student's academic success and well-being.**

Effective Leaders

a) Recruit, hire, support, develop, and retain effective and caring teachers and other professional staff and form them into an educationally effective faculty.
b) Plan for and manage staff turnover and succession, providing opportunities for effective induction and mentoring of new personnel.
c) Develop teachers' and staff members' professional knowledge, skills, and practice through differentiated opportunities for learning and growth, guided by understanding of professional and adult learning and development.
d) Foster continuous improvement of individual and collective instructional capacity to achieve outcomes envisioned for each student.
e) Deliver actionable feedback about instruction and other professional practice through valid, research-anchored systems of supervision and evaluation to support the development of teachers' and staff members' knowledge, skills, and practice.
f) Empower and motivate teachers and staff to the highest levels of professional practice and to continuous learning and improvement.
g) Develop the capacity, opportunities, and support for teacher leadership and leadership from other members of the school community.
h) Promote the personal and professional health, well-being, and work-life balance of faculty and staff.
i) Tend to their own learning and effectiveness through reflection, study, and improvement, maintaining a healthy work-life balance.

STANDARD 7: PROFESSIONAL COMMUNITY FOR TEACHERS AND STAFF

> **Effective educational leaders foster a professional community of teachers and other professional staff to promote each student's academic success and well-being.**

Effective Leaders

a) Develop workplace conditions for teachers and other professional staff that promote effective professional development, practice, and student learning.
b) Empower and entrust teachers and staff with collective responsibility for meeting the academic, social, emotional, and physical needs of each student, pursuant to the mission, vision, and core values of the school.
c) Establish and sustain a professional culture of engagement and commitment to shared vision, goals, and objectives pertaining to the education of the whole child; high expectations for professional work; ethical and equitable practice; trust and open communication; collaboration, collective efficacy, and continuous individual and organizational learning and improvement.
d) Promote mutual accountability among teachers and other professional staff for each student's success and the effectiveness of the school as a whole.
e) Develop and support open, productive, caring, and trusting working relationships among leaders, faculty, and staff to promote professional capacity and the improvement of practice.
f) Design and implement job-embedded and other opportunities for professional learning collaboratively with faculty and staff.
g) Provide opportunities for collaborative examination of practice, collegial feedback, and collective learning.
h) Encourage faculty-initiated improvement of programs and practices.

STANDARD 8: MEANINGFUL ENGAGEMENT OF FAMILIES AND COMMUNITY

> Effective educational leaders engage families and the community in meaningful, reciprocal, and mutually beneficial ways to promote each student's academic success and well-being.

Effective Leaders

a) Are approachable, accessible, and welcoming to families and members of the community.
b) Create and sustain positive, collaborative, and productive relationships with families and the community for the benefit of students.
c) Engage in regular and open two-way communication with families and the community about the school, students, needs, problems, and accomplishments.

d) Maintain a presence in the community to understand its strengths and needs, develop productive relationships, and engage its resources for the school.
e) Create means for the school community to partner with families to support student learning in and out of school.
f) Understand, value, and employ the community's cultural, social, intellectual, and political resources to promote student learning and school improvement.
g) Develop and provide the school as a resource for families and the community.
h) Advocate for the school and district, and for the importance of education and student needs and priorities to families and the community.
i) Advocate publicly for the needs and priorities of students, families, and the community.
j) Build and sustain productive partnerships with public and private sectors to promote school improvement and student learning.

STANDARD 9: OPERATIONS AND MANAGEMENT

> Effective educational leaders manage school operations and resources to promote each student's academic success and well-being.

Effective Leaders

a) Institute, manage, and monitor operations and administrative systems that promote the mission and vision of the school.
b) Strategically manage staff resources, assigning and scheduling teachers and staff to roles and responsibilities that optimize their professional capacity to address each student's learning needs.
c) Seek, acquire, and manage fiscal, physical, and other resources to support curriculum, instruction, and assessment; student learning community; professional capacity and community; and family and community engagement.
d) Are responsible, ethical, and accountable stewards of the school's monetary and nonmonetary resources, engaging in effective budgeting and accounting practices.
e) Protect teachers' and other staff members' work and learning from disruption.
f) Employ technology to improve the quality and efficiency of operations and management.

g) Develop and maintain data and communication systems to deliver actionable information for classroom and school improvement.
h) Know, comply with, and help the school community understand local, state, and federal laws, rights, policies, and regulations so as to promote student success.
i) Develop and manage relationships with feeder and connecting schools for enrollment management and curricular and instructional articulation.
j) Develop and manage productive relationships with the central office and school board.
k) Develop and administer systems for fair and equitable management of conflict among students, faculty and staff, leaders, families, and community.
l) Manage governance processes and internal and external politics toward achieving the school's mission and vision.

STANDARD 10: SCHOOL IMPROVEMENT

> Effective educational leaders act as agents of continuous improvement to promote each student's academic success and well-being.

Effective Leaders

a) Seek to make school more effective for each student, teachers and staff, families, and the community.
b) Use methods of continuous improvement to achieve the vision, fulfil the mission, and promote the core values of the school.
c) Prepare the school and the community for improvement, promoting readiness, an imperative for improvement, instilling mutual commitment and accountability, and developing the knowledge, skills, and motivation to succeed in improvement.
d) Engage others in an ongoing process of evidence-based inquiry, learning, strategic goal setting, planning, implementation, and evaluation for continuous school and classroom improvement.
e) Employ situationally-appropriate strategies for improvement, including transformational and incremental, adaptive approaches and attention to different phases of implementation.
f) Assess and develop the capacity of staff to assess the value and applicability of emerging educational trends and the findings of research for the school and its improvement.

g) Develop technically appropriate systems of data collection, management, analysis, and use, connecting as needed to the district office and external partners for support in planning, implementation, monitoring, feedback, and evaluation.
h) Adopt a systems perspective and promote coherence among improvement efforts and all aspects of school organization, programs, and services.
i) Manage uncertainty, risk, competing initiatives, and politics of change with courage and perseverance, providing support and encouragement, and openly communicating the need for, process for, and outcomes of improvement efforts.
j) Develop and promote leadership among teachers and staff for inquiry, experimentation and innovation, and initiating and implementing improvement.

PSEL CHANGES

One of the major additions to PSEL is the stronger emphasis on student learning. The NPBEA[5] notes that it is critical for leaders to have a pertinent curriculum and teachers in place and that it is as critical for leaders to embed attention to students in their work. All of the data analyses, teacher observations, and central office observations must focus on excelling learning for students. A strong link is essential between student learning and the educational leader.

Human relationship in leadership as it relates to teaching and student learning is another area stressed in PSEL. Although completed in 1920, the Hawthorne studies suggest the value of human relationships in an electrical company. However, the importance of human relationships is being stressed more and more in many work environments. NPBEL[6] also suggest that the PSEL are grounded in the present but are aspirational as well. PSEL challenge educational leaders and attempt to inspire leaders based on what has been accomplished.

It can also be observed that in the ISLLC 2008 and ELCC 2011 Standards there were six core standards. Internship is included in ELCC due to the focus on leadership preparation programs. There are ten PSEL. The major additions are discussed previously. In the following chart, the focus on student learning in PSEL is obvious with three standards (4, 6, and 7) addressing teaching, learning, and curriculum. PSEL 3, 5, and 10 are additions. In many of the PSEL, the indirect links to human relationships are evident. For instance, in PSEL 5 and 7, there is the verbiage "community," which is the link for the leader to facilitate relationships.

Table 1.2. A Comparison of the PSEL 2015, ISLLC 2008, and ELCC 2011

PSEL 2015	ISLLC 2008	ELCC 2011
Standard 1: Mission, Vision, and Core Values Effective educational leaders develop, advocate, and enact a shared mission, vision, and core values of high-quality education and academic success and well-being of each student.	**Standard 1: Vision of Learning** Facilitating the development, articulation, and implementation, and stewardship of a vision of learning that is shared and supported by the school community.	**Standard 1** Candidates who complete the program are educational leaders who have the knowledge and ability to promote the success of all students by facilitating the development, articulation, implementation, and stewardship of a school or district **vision** of learning supported by the school community.
Standard 4: Curriculum, Instruction, and Assessment Effective educational leaders develop and support intellectually rigorous and coherent systems of curriculum, instruction, and assessment to promote each student's academic success and well-being. **Standard 6: Professional Capacity of School Personnel** Effective educational leaders develop the professional capacity and practice of school personnel to promote each student's academic success and well-being. **Standard 7: Professional Community for Teachers and Staff** Effective educational leaders foster a professional community of teachers and other professional staff to promote each student's academic success and well-being.	**Standard 2: The Culture of Teaching and Learning** Advocating, nurturing, and sustaining a school culture and instructional program conducive to student learning and professional growth.	**Standard 2** Candidates who complete the program are educational leaders who have the knowledge and ability to promote the success of all students by promoting a positive school culture, providing an effective **instructional program**, applying best practice to student learning, and designing comprehensive professional growth plans for staff.

(Continued)

Table 1.2. (Continued)

PSEL 2015	ISLLC 2008	ELCC 2011
Standard 9: Operations and Management Effective educational leaders manage school operations and resources to promote each student's academic success and well-being.	**Standard 3: Management of Learning** Ensuring management of the organizations, operations, and resources for a safe, efficient, and effective learning environment.	**Standard 3** Candidates who complete the program are educational leaders who have the knowledge and ability to promote the success of all students by **managing the organization, operations,** and resources in a way that promotes a safe, efficient, and effective learning environment.
Standard 8: Meaningful Engagement of Families and Community Effective educational leaders engage families and the community in meaningful, reciprocal, and mutually beneficial ways to promote each student's academic success and well-being.	**Standard 4: Relations with the Broader Community to Foster Learning** Collaborating with families and community members, responding to diverse community interests and needs, and mobilizing community resources.	**Standard 4** Candidates who complete the program are educational leaders who have the knowledge and ability to promote the success of all students by collaborating **with families and other community members,** responding to diverse community interests and needs, and mobilizing community resources.
Standard 2: Ethics and Professional Norms Effective educational leaders act ethically and according to professional norms to promote each student's academic success and well-being.	**Standard 5: Integrity, Fairness, and Ethics in Learning** Acting with integrity, fairness, and in an ethical manner.	**Standard 5** Candidates who complete the program are educational leaders who have the knowledge and ability to promote the success of all students by acting with **integrity, fairly, and in an ethical manner.**

Standard 6:
The Political, Social, Economic, Legal, and Cultural Context of Learning
Understanding, responding to, and influencing the larger political, economic, legal and cultural contexts

Not related directly to any 2008 ISLLC or 2011 ELCC standards
Not related directly to any 2008 ISLLC or 2011 ELCC standards

Standard 10: School Improvement Effective educational leaders act as agents of continuous improvement to promote each student's academic success and well-being

Standard 3: Equity and Cultural Responsiveness
Effective educational leaders strive for equity of educational opportunity and culturally responsive practices to promote each student's academic success and well-being.

Standard 5: Community of Care and Support for Students
Effective educational leaders cultivate an inclusive, caring, and supportive school community that promotes the academic success and well-being of each student.

Standard 6
Candidates who complete the program are educational leaders who have the knowledge and ability to promote the success of all students by understanding, responding to, and influencing the **larger political, social, economic, legal, and cultural context**.

According to the National Association of Secondary School Principals (NASSP) PSEL has a greater emphasis on "each" student. PSEL provide for a systemic view of leadership, and have suggested areas of elevation and elaboration, which are as follows:

- Mission, vision, core values;
- Ethics, equity, and cultural responsiveness;
- Academic press/rigor and community of care of support of students;
- Development of teachers and professional staff, and professional community and working conditions;
- Meaningful engagement of families and community; and
- Leadership for school improvement.

There are several other observations regarding PSEL as well. Shapiro and colleagues[7] noted that there is a greater emphasis on ethics, and there is one standard—Standard 2—devoted to ethics and professional norms; and ethics is addressed in Standards 1, 5, 6, and 7 of PSEL. This notion is discussed further in chapter 2.

NOTES

1. Anthes, K. *What's Happening in School and District Leadership?* Denver, CO: Education Commission of the State: MetLife Foundation. 2005. Print.
2. Anthes, K. *What's Happening in School and District Leadership?*
3. ISLLC. Retrieved from http://www.umsl.edu/~mpea/Pages/About ISSLC/.
4. Educational Leadership Constituent Council. National Policy Board for Educational Administration. Retrieved from http://www.npbea.org/.
5. National Policy Board for Educational Administration. National Educational Leadership Preparation Standards. Retrieved from http://www.npbea.org/.
6. National Policy Board for Educational Administration. National Educational Leadership Preparation Standards. Retrieved from http:///www.npbea.org/.
7. Shapiro, Joan Poliner, and Stefkovich, Jacqueline Anne. *Ethical Leadership and Decision Making in Education: Applying Theoretical Perspectives to Complex Dilemmas.* 3rd ed. Mahwah, NJ: L. Routledge, 2010. Print.

Chapter 2

Professional Standards for Educational Leaders: Standards 1, 2, 3, and 10: "The Drivers"

Vision Resources—http://teaching.about.com/od/admin/ss/Educational-Leadership-Philosophy.htm and http://www.ascd.org/publications/books/107042/chapters/Developing-a-Vision-and-a-Mission.aspx

In the PSEL, Standards 1, 2, 3, and 10 are referred to as the "drivers." Standard 1 is Mission, Vision, and Core Values. Standard 2 is Ethics and Professional Norms. Standard 3 is Equity and Cultural Responsiveness; and Standard 10 is School Improvement. The importance of a vision in schools has long been noted as evident in the 1996 version of the ISLLC. In the PSEL, mission and core values are added.

The mission can be viewed as the "driver" in working toward the vision, and this must be done with a core set of values—the notions that are nonnegotiable as a part of the culture. The nonnegotiables align with ethics—Standard 2. It is essential for ethical dispositions to be exhibited at all times, which require professionals to be responsive to the needs of others in decision making related to every aspect of schools while striving for the promotion of equitable opportunities for all students—PSEL 3. This is so critical for all aspects for schools but particularly Standard 10—School Improvement.

Standard 1 has seven elements, five of which include vision. The following are the PSEL elements for Standard 1 that include vision and effective leaders:

- In collaboration with members of the school and the community and using relevant data, develop and promote a vision for the school on the successful learning and development of each child and on instructional and organizational practices that promote such success.
- Strategically develop, implement, and evaluate actions to achieve the vision for the school.

Table 2.1. PSEL Standards

	2008 ISLLC	2011 ELCC
Standard 1: Mission, Vision, and Core Values Effective educational leaders develop, advocate, and enact a shared mission, vision, and core values of high-quality education and academic success and well-being of each student.	**Standard 1: Vision of Learning** Facilitating the development, articulation, implementation, and stewardship of a vision of learning that is shared and supported by the school community.	**Standard 1** Candidates who complete the program are educational leaders who have the knowledge and ability to promote the success of all students by facilitating the development, articulation, implementation, and stewardship of a school or district **vision** of learning supported by the school community.
Standard 2: Ethics and Professional Norms Effective educational leaders act ethically and according to professional norms to promote each student's academic success and well-being.	**Standard 5: Integrity, Fairness, and Ethics in Learning** Acting with integrity, fairness, and in an ethical manner.	**Standard 5** Candidates who complete the program are educational leaders who have the knowledge and ability to promote the success of all students by acting with **integrity, fairly, and in an ethical manner.**
	Standard 6: The Political, Social, Economic, Legal, and Cultural Context of Learning Understanding, responding to, and influencing the larger political, economic, legal, and cultural contexts	**Standard 6** Candidates who complete the program are educational leaders who have the knowledge and ability to promote the success of all students by understanding, responding to, and influencing the **larger political, social, economic, legal, and cultural context.**
Standard 3: Equity and Cultural Responsiveness Effective educational leaders strive for equity of educational opportunity and culturally responsive practices to promote each student's academic success and well-being. **Standard 10: School Improvement** Effective educational leaders act as agents of continuous improvement to promote each student's academic success and well-being	Not related directly to any 2008 ISLLC or 2011 ELCC Standards	

- Review the school's mission and vision and adjust them to changing expectations and opportunities for the school, and changing needs and situations of students.
- Develop shared understanding of and commitment to mission, vision, and core values within the school and the community.
- Model and pursue the school's mission, vision, and core values in all aspects of leadership.

Vision and mission have been used interchangeably. However, there is a difference. A vision describes the goals for the future, whereas mission includes the founding purpose. The instructional values or public commitments are often included in missions, while the loftiest ideals, organizational values, and long-term objectives are included in visions. Generally, visions describe the end goal, and missions provide the commitments and actions needed to achieve the visions (http://edglossary.org/mission-and-vision/).

It is noteworthy that in Element 2 of PSEL 1 (*In collaboration with members of the school and the community and using relevant data, develop and promote a vision for the school on the successful learning and development of each child and on instructional and organizational practices that promote such success*) it has several embedded implications for the leader. According to Razik and Swanson (2000)[1] one of the most important responsibilities of any leader is to establish a vision and to invite others to share in the development. It is important that the vision be developed in collaboration with members of the school community.

The concept of a shared vision is indicative of involvement in the process and "buy-in" from the school community in the creating of the vision (Elements 2, 3, 4, 5, 6, and 7). The teachers and other employees and, to some extent, the students have to assist with implementation of the vision; therefore, it is important to involve them in its development early. Employees of the school and school district are often referred to as the internal publics, while the parents and other community members are the external publics. Both internal and external publics (stakeholders) should be involved with vision processes and school improvement.

In addition to involving stakeholders, relevant data should be used (Elements 2 and 4). Gabriel and Farmer[2] suggest that data should be shared first with the oversight team, and that it is important to use the most relevant, current data. It is equally important for all stakeholders to have an understanding of the data and a comfort level with its meaning.

Gabriel and Farmer[3] also note that the sharing and understanding of the data provide the foundation to build on along with the understanding of the current functioning levels of the school outlining both the need and direction for change. Obviously, student learning and the promotion of student success are the goals in the visioning review processes and in establishing the vision.

In Element 4 of Standard 1 of PSEL, it is noted that in addition to strategically developing the vision, it must be implemented with evaluation of actions. It is therefore necessary for ongoing communication, assessment, and reevaluation of the vision to occur with its implementation. Collaboration among the stakeholders becomes essential. The communication and collaboration help the school leader in facilitating the shared understanding and the continuous pursuit of both the vision and mission.

The connection of the vision to the classroom heightens the attention of school leaders and others to school improvement (Standard 10 of PSEL). The vision planning and school improvement planning are both linked to the classroom and are based on the same kinds of data.

In addition, several of the elements of school improvement relate directly to elements embedded in the vision elements (Elements 1, 2, 3, 4, and 5). As it relates to the discussion, the vision is viewed as developing the component of school improvement. Not only is there an instructional component to school improvement, there are technical, systemic, and managerial components as noted in the elements of Standard 10 of PSEL as well. There are ten constructs, which are categorized as instructional (i), managerial (m), technical (t), and/or systemic (s) as follows.

Effective Leaders

- Seek to make school more effective for each student, teachers and staff, families, and the community (s).
- Use methods of continuous improvement to achieve the vision, fulfill the mission, and promote the core values of the school (i).
- Prepare the school and the community for improvement, promoting readiness, an imperative for improvement, instilling mutual commitment and accountability, and developing the knowledge, skills, and motivation to succeed in improvement (s).
- Engage others in an ongoing process of evidence-based inquiry, learning, strategic goal setting, planning, implementation, and evaluation for continuous school and classroom improvement (s).
- Employ situationally-appropriate strategies for improvement, including transformational and incremental, adaptive approaches and attention to different phases of implementation (m, t).
- Assess and develop the capacity of staff to assess the value and applicability of emerging educational trends and the findings of research for the school and its improvement (s, m, t).
- Develop technically appropriate systems of data collection, management, analysis, and use, connecting as needed to the district office and external partners for support in planning, implementation, monitoring, feedback, and evaluation (s).

- Adopt a systems perspective and promote coherence among improvement efforts and all aspects of school organization, programs, and services (s).
- Manage uncertainty, risk, competing initiatives, and politics of change with courage and perseverance, providing support and encouragement, and openly communicating the need for, process for, and outcomes of improvement efforts (m).
- Develop and promote leadership among teachers and staff for inquiry, experimentation and innovation, and initiating and implementing improvement (i).

Numerous programs and strategies for improving schools have been implemented over the years. There are commonalities and differences in the programs and strategies targeting school improvement; however, one common theme in the recent programs and strategies is the importance of the role of the school leader. School improvement and student learning are mentioned throughout the publication and are essential parts of PSEL. Many of the school improvement practices are tied to accountability. The importance of accountability will be discussed in the concluding chapter.

The following (figures 2.1 to 2.6) are sample school improvement planning models/processes:

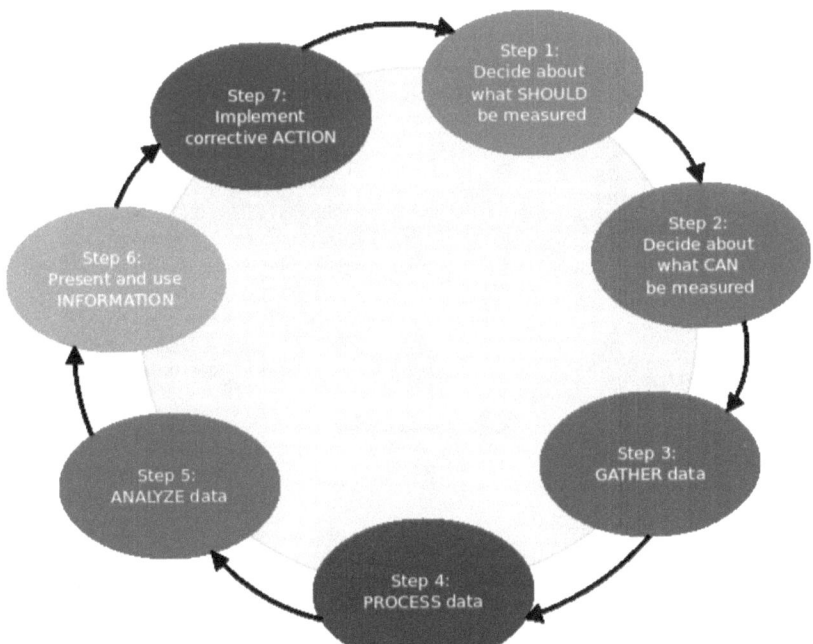

Figure 2.1. 7-Step Continual Service Improvement Process. *Source*: ICCLAB. *7 Step Continual Service Improvement Process*. Digital image. *Service Engineering Research*. Zurich University of Applied Sciences, October 14, 2016. https://blog.zhaw.ch/icclab/how-to-apply-the-7-step-continual-service-improvement-process-in-a-cloud-computing-environment/. October 14, 2016.

SchoolStat PDSA Continuous Improvement Model

Stage	Plan	Do	Study	Act
Where	SchoolStat Meeting	School	SchoolStat Meeting	School
Steps	• Data analysis • Identify opportunities for improvement (OFIs) • Identify root causes • Share existing strategies and/or design new strategies • Design action steps • Design an evaluation plan	• Implement action steps defined in the PLAN stage	• Monitor implementation • Evaluate effect against defined desired outcome in PLAN stage • Revise action steps, refine, abandon strategy (as indicated)	• Implement revised action as defined in STUDY stage • Repeat cycle

Figure 2.2. Continuous Improvement Model. *Source*: SchoolStat. *SchoolStat PDSA Continuous Improvement Model*. Digital image. SchoolStat. N.p., 2016. https://www2.ed.gov/admins/tchrqual/learn/nclbsummit/thornton/thornton.pdf. October 14, 2016.

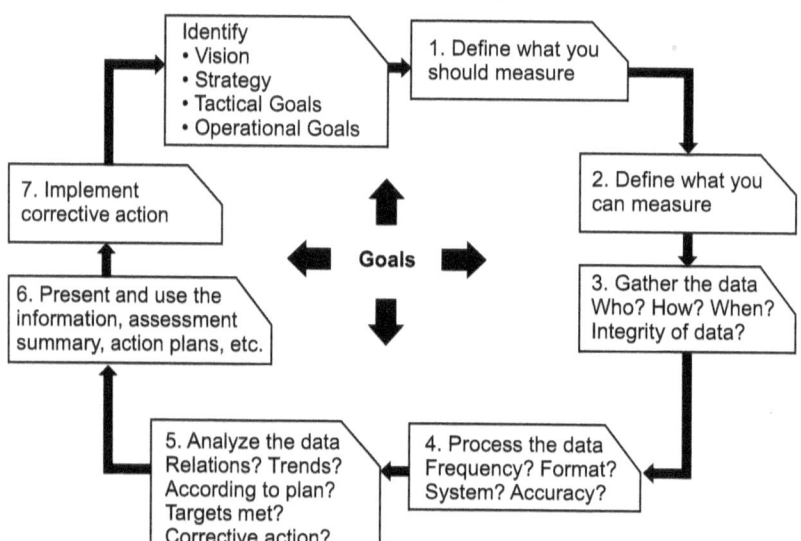

Figure 2.3. 7-Step Improvement Process. *Source*: Split Horizon. *Figure 6: The 7-Step Improvement Process*. Digital image. *Split Horizon*. N.p., 2016. https://blog.zhaw.ch/icclab/how-to-apply-the-7-step-continual-service-improvement-process-in-a-cloud-computing-environment/. October 14, 2016.

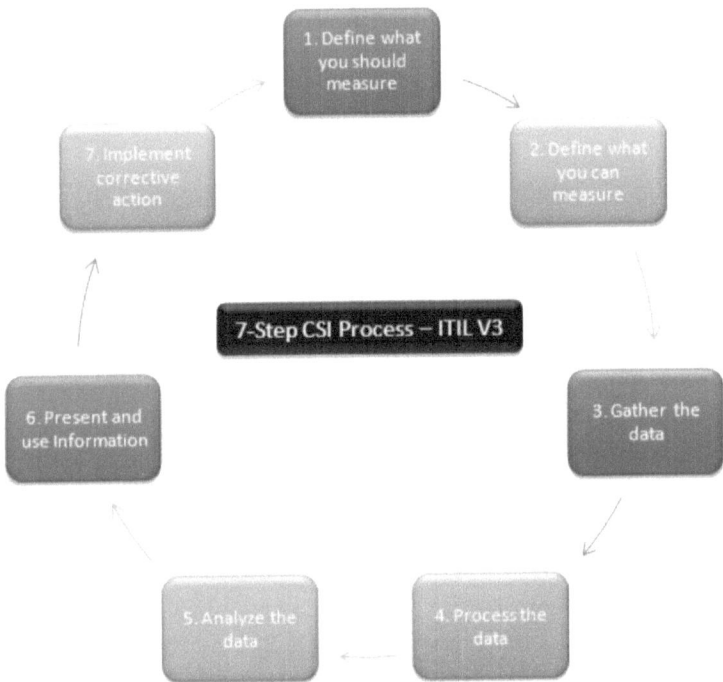

Figure 2.4. 7-Step Continual Service Process. *Source*: Syed, Z. *7-Step CSI Process - ITIL V3*. Digital image. *SQew Notepad*. N.p., September 25 2011. http://mayodeleheath.blogspot.com/2015/01/itil-v3-foundation-continual-service.html. October 14, 2016.

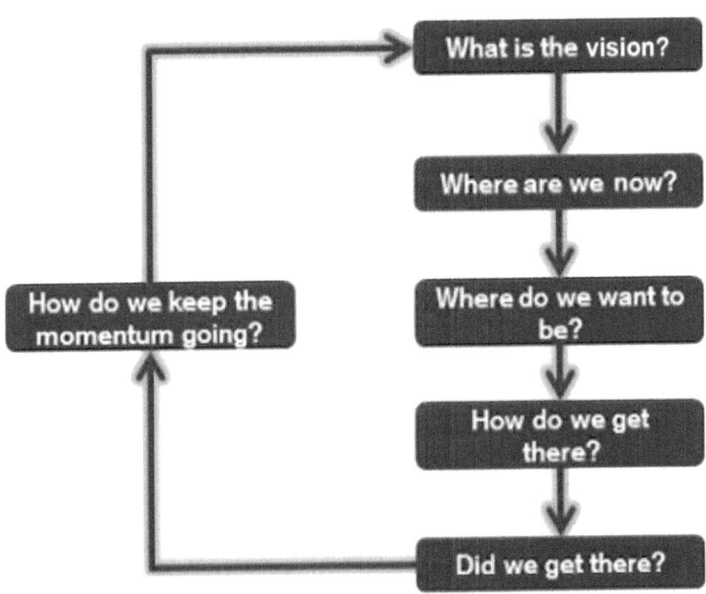

Figure 2.5. The Continual Service Improvement Model. *Source*: VijayaKumar, Anad. *The Continual Service Improvement Model*. Digital image. *Learn ITIL V3*. N.p., December 29, 2011. http://learnitilv3.blogspot.com/2011/12/continual-service-improvement-model.html. October 14, 2016.

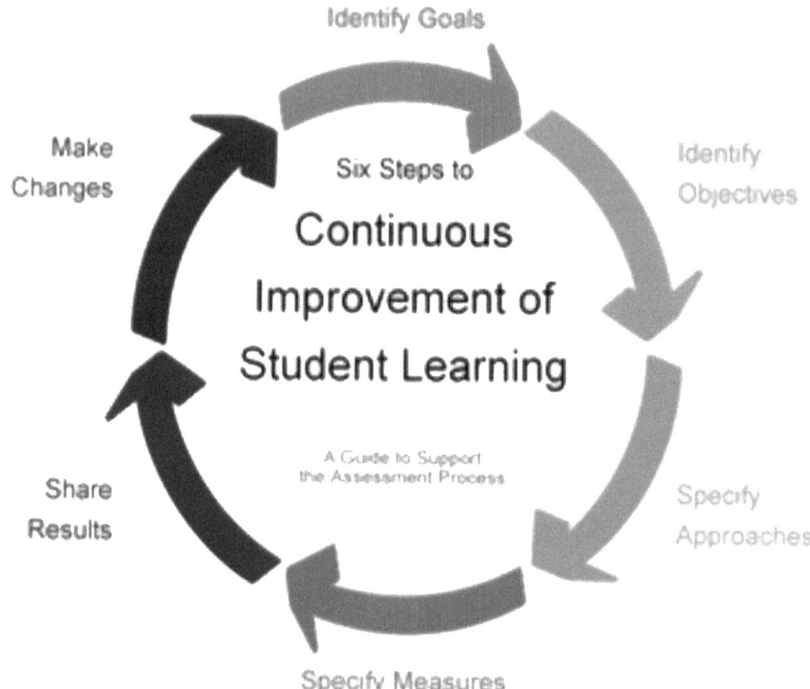

Figure 2.6. Six Steps to Continuous Improvement of Student Learning. *Source*: Kent State University. *Six Steps to Continuous Improvement of Student Learning*. Digital image. *Elementary Math Work Stations*. N.p., 2016. https://lifehacks.io/six-steps-to-continuous-improvement-of-student-learning/. October 14, 2016.

Another "driver" is Standard 2 of PSEL: Ethics and Professional Norms.

STANDARD 2: ETHICS AND PROFESSIONAL NORMS

> **Effective educational leaders act ethically and according to professional norms to promote each student's academic success and well-being.**

Effective Leaders

a) Act ethically and professionally in personal conduct, relationships with others, decision-making, stewardship of the school's resources, and all aspects of school leadership.

b) Act according to and promote the professional norms of integrity, fairness, transparency, trust, collaboration, perseverance, learning, and continuous improvement.
c) Place children at the center of education and accept responsibility for each student's academic success and well-being.
d) Safeguard and promote the values of democracy, individual freedom and responsibility, equity, social justice, community, and diversity.
e) Lead with interpersonal and communication skill, social-emotional insight, and understanding of all students' and staff members' backgrounds and cultures.
f) Provide moral direction for the school and promote ethical and professional behavior among faculty and staff.

The elements of Standard 2 directly or indirectly address "ethics" and professional norms. Ethics should be embedded in every aspect of schools and work environments. Ethical behavior is noted in the elements for personal conduct (Elements 1, 2, 3, 4, 5, and 6 of PSEL 1), relationship with others (Element 1 of PSEL 1), decision making (Element 1 of PSEL 1), management of resources (Element 1 of PSEL 1), and other aspects of leadership (Elements 1, 2, 3, 4, 5, and 6 of PSEL 1).

According to Shapiro and colleagues,[4] a number of educational professional organizations have developed ethical codes. States have also outlined codes of ethics and mandate that employees be current through mandatory professional development.

In the next paragraph, the principles from the American Association of Educators are presented. However, other organizations with ethical codes include but are not limited to the American Association of University Professors, the American Psychological Association, the Association of School Business Officials, the Association for Supervision and Curriculum Development, and the National Education Association.

The American Association of Educators has established four principles in a code of ethics to create learning environments to ensure learning for student, to have educators accept responsibility that all children have a right to education, and to have educators make conscientious efforts to exemplify standards that parallel Standard 2 of PSEL. The following are the ethical principles:

- Principle I is ethical conduct toward students.
- Principle II is ethical conduct toward practices and performances.
- Principle III is ethical conduct toward professional colleagues.
- Principle IV is ethical conduct toward parents and the community.

Most of the work that leaders and educators do is with students that often require a great deal of interaction. The need for educators to conduct all interactions with students in an ethical way is essential. Included in Element 3 of Standard 2 of PSEL is that students should be at the center of education. Students are the priority. In addition, educators have a responsibility in ensuring the success and well-being of students. There is a concept in school law—in loco parentis. The implication is that educators act in the "place of parents," while children are in the care of educators.

Decision making and exhibiting appropriate professional norms and dispositions (PSEL 2) are ongoing for school leaders. Harvey and Ventura[5] presented five key principles pertinent to "doing what is right." The principles are the following: words to live by are just words unless you live by them; you are what you do; everything you do counts; the golden rule is still pure gold; and character is key. There are nine tenets of character. Harvey and Ventura[6] suggest that commitment, honesty, accountability, respect, appropriate attitude, courage, trust, ethics and integrity, and responsibility are the pillars of character.

Element 2 of PSEL Standard 2: Ethics and Professional Norms includes the pillars of character presented by Harvey and Ventura.[7] It is noted in the construct that effective leaders act accordingly to promote the norms of integrity, fairness, transparency, trust, collaboration, perseverance, learning, and continuous improvement. Transparency is a concept that many leaders profess; however, exhibiting is more of a challenge. Employees want to perceive that there are no hidden agendas in work environments that closely align with how much trust is shared. The absence/presence of trust can definitely impact culture.

The cultures of schools are directly impacted by how much people trust each other, how professional norms are promoted, and many of the other concepts embedded in ethics. Culture is cited and included in many of the PSEL Standard elements, and it is described in many ways. Several of the perspectives will be addressed as aligned with the standard elements for emphasizing the rules of school leaders pertinent to culture. As early as 1957, Selznick noted that culture provides the distinctive identify for/of schools.

In 1968, Taiguiri[8] provided four dimensions of climate inclusive of culture referred to as the Taiguiran Typology of Climate. The dimensions are ecology (building characteristics, school size); milieu (student and teacher characteristics); social systems (social interactions); and culture (belief systems and values). Hoy and Miskel[9] describe culture as the norms, shared beliefs, rituals, and assumptions of the organization. There are several researchers who indicate the importance of positive cultures in schools, and it is also noted that the school leaders play pivotal roles in monitoring and shaping the culture.

Marzano, Waters, and McNulty[10] defined twenty-one responsibilities of school leaders and correlated the responsibilities to student achievement. The role of the leader linked to culture is correlated highly as impacting student achievement. Brewster and Railsback[11] note the importance of building trust in the publication *Building Trusting Relationships for School Improvement: Implications for Principals and Teachers*. They note several perspectives and essential elements of trust.

In addition, they provide the following practical suggestions for principals to build trust between teachers:

- Demonstrate personal integrity;
- Show that you care;
- Be accessible;
- Facilitate and model effective communication;
- Involve staff in decision making;
- Celebrate experimentation and support risk;
- Express value for dissenting views;
- Reduce teachers' sense of vulnerability;
- Ensure that teachers have basic resource; and
- Be prepared to replace ineffective teachers.

They also note that leaders have to facilitate trust among teachers. The following are the strategies to build trust among teachers:

- Engage the full faculty in activities and discussion related to the school's mission, vision, and core values;
- Make the new teachers feel welcome;
- Create and support meaningful opportunities for teachers to work collaboratively;
- Identify ways to increase and/or improve faculty communication;
- Make relationship building a priority; and
- Choose a professional development model that promotes relationship building.

The notions stressed by Brewster and Railsback[12] linked to culture is also noted by Hoy and Miskel[13] and Bryk and Schnedider.[14] Culture is an important concept as linked and aligned to many aspects of schools.

The additional elements of Standard 2 of PSEL require school leaders to:

- Safeguard and promote the values of democracy, individual freedom and responsibility, equity, social justice, community, and diversity (Element 4, PSEL 2).

- Lead with interpersonal and communication skill, social-emotional insight, and understanding of all students' and staff members' backgrounds and cultures (Element 5, PSEL 2).
- Provide moral direction for the school and promote ethical and professional behavior among faculty and staff (Element 6, PSEL 2).

These elements can be achieved by following ethical codes and/or resolving clashes of codes of ethics, which will be elaborated on. Shapiro and colleagues[15] discuss a very important point pertinent to ethics related to the potential clashes that are vital to the elements of Standard 2 of PSEL listed earlier. Individuals often develop their professional and personal codes of ethics that are based on observations of various ethical models.

Four kinds of clashes can occur. The professional and personal clashing of the codes of ethics is the first clash. The second is clashes can occur within professional codes—codes may be different from professional association to professional association. The third type of clash occurs among leaders when leaders have varying perspectives, and the fourth type occurs when the leader's personal and professional codes of ethics are different from what is expected by the school community.[16]

These clashes can be resolved by leaders who revert to PSEL and make decisions on the basis of "the best interest" of students. This is the manner by which morality is embraced (Element 6, PSEL 2), leadership utilizing effective communication (Element 5, PSEL 2), and safeguarding to promote democracy (Element 4, PSEL 2). It will require the leader to engage in participatory decision making—communicating effectively with teachers, parents, students, and other stakeholders.

The central goal for leaders and all educators pertinent particularly to ethics is a concept mentioned earlier in the chapter. Educators must act/respond "in loco parentis": in the place of parents as it relates to school children (Element 3, PSEL 2).

It is important to highlight that in PSEL ethics is a "stand-alone standard": an entire standard is devoted to ethics. In addition, ethics is addressed in Standard 1 of PSEL as linked to core values; Standard 3 of PSEL as linked to equity and culture; Standard 5 of PSEL as linked to supporting students and the community; and Standards 6 and 7 as it relates to supporting personnel. It is a safe assertion that there is heightened emphasis on ethics in PSEL that will have implications for future leaders.

The last PSEL, referred to as a "driver," is Standard 3: Equity and Cultural Responsiveness. Many of the elements in Standard 3 are addressed in Standard 2 pertinent to Ethics, while also addressing the culture of students and other diverse factors, which include the following:

- Ensuring that each student is treated fairly, respectfully, and with an understanding of each student's culture and context.
- Recognizing, respecting, and employing each student's strengths, diversity, and culture as assets for teaching and learning.
- Developing student policies and addressing student misconduct in a positive, fair, and unbiased manner.
- Promoting the preparation of students to live productively in and contributing to the diverse cultural contexts of a global society.
- Acting with cultural competence and responsiveness in their interactions, decision making, and practice.
- Addressing matters of equity and cultural responsiveness in all aspects of leadership.

The production function research that began in 1966[17] focused on the impact of school variables on achievement. This notion is raised because there are many concepts aligned with this research for equity and diversity of students that leaders should facilitate. Many of the elements of Standard 3 align with the principles of equity and diversity.

Most recent production research suggests that school variables such as expenditure, teacher background, and class size impact achievement. These findings suggest the need for school leaders to ensure that both human and economic resources are available to all students accounting for diversity.

A case study from the second edition of *Passing the Leadership Test* is provided next. Most of the PSEL Standards are embedded in this case. Discussions are appropriate for aligning the PSEL to the case. There are questions that follow the case, and standard alignment is included next to the questions to make the link to the PSEL.

CASE 1: PREPARING FOR A NEW LEADERSHIP ROLE

PSEL 1–10

Case Scenario: Karl Jones is still ecstatic over his appointment as the new principal at Jonestown Middle School. There is still a month to go before he will actually begin the job and two and one-half months before the school year starts. This appointment will be Karl's first principal's position, although he served as an assistant principal at the other middle school in Jonestown.

Bob Smith is the person Karl is replacing. Bob had been principal for the previous twelve years. He inherited a school that had one of the lowest performance ratings in the state. From 1999 through 2009 Jonestown Middle School had experienced steady measurable growth in student performance as determined by increased standardized test scores and reduced student absences.

When Bob Smith arrived at Jonestown the school performance score was 36; the percentage of students successfully passing their state assessment tests was 31, and on an average, only 41 percent of the students enrolled attended school each day.

By 2009, the school performance score was 84 percent, with 77 percent of students passing state assessment tests, and average daily attendance at 91 percent. However, after ten years of consistent gains, percentages on all three metrics had declined two consecutive years.

Karl Jones's charge upon appointment was simple: Reverse the trend! He already had some ideas he was prepared to implement. However, as he prepared plans and strategies to implement his ideas an incident occurred at his former school that awakened him to another reality. Simply put, that reality is: School leaders charged with school reform and turnaround have to be prepared to deal with unexpected problem issues, especially in the absence of policies that cover those issues.

Although he did not have all of the details, Karl Jones had these facts about the incident that took place at his former school. An eighth-grade student there had used his smartphone to download and forward pornographic material to ten of his friends.

Several of those friends in turn forwarded the material to their friends and before anyone knew what was happening 89 percent of the sixth-, seventh-, and eighth-grade students at the school had received and saved the porn material on their personal electronic devices, including smartphones and personal computers.

As soon as the principal of Karl's former school became aware of the incident, he enlisted the help of Jonestown City Police and confiscated the smartphones and personal computers of all the students who had them at school. Karl had no other information. The only policy in place at the school forbade students to use school computers to view or download any illicit material.

What surprised Karl Jones the most however, and as reported on the local television station, was not the fact that middle school students were viewing porn material but the fact that the large number of parents were objecting to the confiscation of their children's electronic devices.

Karl Jones was preparing to implement reform and turnaround measures at his new school. However, he could not help reflecting on how he would approach such an incident at his new school if there was no school or district policy to address it. He reasoned, "My reform initiative now must be forward thinking to the extent of developing school policies that, driven by rapid changes in technology, are general and comprehensive enough to encompass such unexpected incidents."

Questions: With reference to the PSEL Standards cited earlier and only the incidents at Karl's old school:

1. Which types of knowledge and understanding are required for the administrator/school leader to address in this case? List at least five and justify each one chosen.
2. Which dispositions are required for the administrator/school leader to address this case? List at least five and justify each one chosen.
3. Which performance indicators should the administrator/school leader apply in this case? List at least five and justify each one chosen.
4. If you were Karl Jones what steps would you take to develop a general technology policy comprehensive enough to cover the next five years?

Elements of the "drivers" are embedded throughout this case. School leaders must have visions for schools (elements of PSEL 1). A common challenge for school leaders is to conduct a needs assessment based on data for the purpose of school improvement (elements of PSEL 10). As leaders work toward school improvement, the other "drivers" are so critical—PSEL 2 and 3. Upholding the principles of ethics and being culturally responsive are critical.

As previously noted, there are concepts in the case that can be linked to all standards of PSEL. In chapter 3, there is a focus on the "core": PSEL 4 and 5. Leaders must develop a community of care and support for learners: PSEL 5; curriculum, instruction, and assessment are at the "core" of the work of the leader as an instructional leader, which is discussed thoroughly in chapter 3.

NOTES

1. Razik, T. A., and Swanson, A. D. *Fundamental Concepts of Educational Leadership*. Belmont, CA: Wadsworth Publishing Company, 2000. Print.

2. Gabriel, J. G., and Farmer, P. C. *How to Help Your School Thrive without Breaking the Bank*. Alexandria, VA: Association for Supervision and Curriculum Development. 2009. Print.

3. Gabriel, J. G., and Farmer, P. C. *How to Help Your School Thrive without Breaking the Bank*.

4. Shapiro, Joan Poliner, and Stefkovich, Jacqueline Anne. *Ethical Leadership and Decision Making in Education.*

5. Harvey, Eric L., and Ventura, Steve. *Walk the Talk.* Dallas, TX: Walk the Talk Company, 2007. Print.

6. Harvey, Eric L., and Ventura, Steve. *Walk the Talk.*

7. Harvey, Eric L., and Ventura, Steve. *Walk the Talk.*

8. Taguiri, R. "The Concept of Organizational Climate." In R. Taguiri and G. H. Litwin (eds.), *Organizational Climate: Exploration of a Concept.* Boston: Division of Research, Graduate School of Business Administration, Harvard University, 1968. Print.

9. Hoy, Wayne K., and Miskel, Cecil G. *Educational Administration: Theory, Research, and Practice.* New York: Random House, 2013. Print.

10. Marzano, Robert J., Waters, Timothy, and McNulty, Brian A. *School Leadership That Works: From Research to Results.* Alexandria, VA: Association for Supervision and Curriculum Development, 2005. Print.

11. Brewster, C., and Railsback, J. *Building Trusting Relationships for School Improvement: Implications for Principals and Teachers.* Portalnad, Oregon: Northwest Regional Educational Laboratory. (September 2003). Print.

12. Brewster, C., and Railsback, J. *Building Trusting Relationships for School Improvement: Implications for Principals and Teachers.*

13. Hoy, Wayne K., and Miskel, Cecil G. *Educational Administration: Theory, Research, and Practice.* New York: Random House, 2013. Print.

14. Bryk, Anthony and Schneider, Barbara. *Trust in Schools: A Core Resource for Improvement* (2002).

15. Shapiro, Joan Poliner, and Stefkovich Jacqueline Anne. *Ethical Leadership and Decision Making in Education.*

16. Shapiro, Joan Poliner, and Stefkovich, Jacqueline Anne. *Ethical Leadership and Decision Making in Education.*

17. Coleman, J. et al. *Equality of Opportunity: Coleman Report.* National Center for Educational Statistics. ED 012 275; Alexandria, VA: Association for Supervision and Curriculum Development, 2005. Print.

Chapter 3

Professional Standards for Educational Leaders: Standards 4 and 5: "The Core"

Standard 4 of PSEL: Curriculum, Instruction, and Assessment and Standard 5 of PSEL: Community of Care and Support for Students are referred to as the "core" for school leaders.

Curriculum, instruction, and assessment are always central to the work of educators. In addition, educators must collaborate and be supported. Hoy and Miskel's[1] social-systems model provides a framework for the roles leaders play in developing and supporting curriculum, instruction, and assessment and cultivating a community for academic success.

The concept from the social system can be applied to society as a whole as well as many work organizations. In addition, the model has many layers and can get very complex. The simplistic version of the model is illustrated in figure 3.1.

Hoy and Miskel[2] suggest that within schools from the perspective of the social-systems model, there are inputs, a transformation process that occurs, followed by outputs. The inputs are focused primarily on what educators do with students to get to the outputs. Inputs include factors such as our environmental constraints, human and capital resources, mission and board policy, and equipment.

The first listed output by Hoy and Miskel[3] is achievement, which is a concept that will be discussed further next. Some of the variables listed for outputs are student related; some are teacher related; others are both student- and teacher-related with implications for others in the school community.

There are so many factors noted as influencing the structural system and influencing the transformational process of the social-systems model; however, the important note is that teaching and learning are included in the transformational process. As previously noted, Hoy and Miskel[4] make a close link to PSEL 4 and 5 with what occurs in the social-systems model

Table 3.1. PSEL Standards

Standard 4: Curriculum, Instruction, and Assessment	Standard 2: The Culture of Teaching and Learning	Standard 2
Effective educational leaders develop and support intellectually rigorous and coherent systems of curriculum, instruction, and assessment to promote each student's academic success and well-being.	Advocating, nurturing, and sustaining a school culture and instructional program conducive to student learning and professional growth.	Candidates who complete the program are educational leaders who have the knowledge and ability to promote the success of all students by promoting a positive school culture, providing an effective **instructional program**, applying best practice to student learning, and designing comprehensive professional growth plans for staff.
Standard 5: Community of Care and Support for Students Effective educational leaders cultivate an inclusive, caring, and supportive school community that promotes the academic success and well-being of each student.		

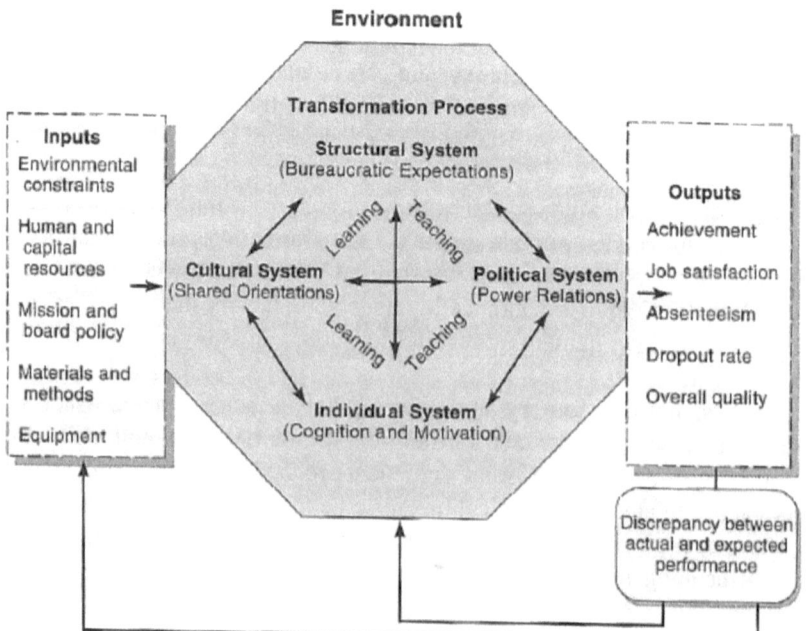

Figure 3.1. Social-Systems Model for Schools. *Source*: Hoy, Wayne K., Miskel, Cecil G., and Tarter, C. John. *Educational Administration: Theory, Research, and Practice*. 9th ed. New York: McGraw-Hill Humanities/Social Sciences/Languages, 2012. Print.

transformational process. Hoy and Miskel[5] describe teaching and learning as being at the technical core of social systems.

Standard 4 of PSEL specifically addresses curriculum, instruction, and assessment. In Table 3.1, the "Core Standards" of PSEL are aligned to the relevant 2008 ISLLC and 2011 ELCC Standards. However, this is the basis for teaching and learning. The elements from PSEL Standard 4 are as follows:

- Implement coherent systems of curriculum, instruction, and assessment that promote the mission, vision, and core values of the school, embody high expectations for student learning, align with academic standards, and are culturally responsive.
- Align and focus systems of curriculum, instruction, and assessment within and across grade levels to promote student academic success, love of learning, the identities and habits of learners, and healthy sense of self.
- Promote instructional practice that is consistent with knowledge of child learning and development, effective pedagogy, and the needs of each student.
- Ensure instructional practice that is intellectually challenging, authentic to student experiences, recognizes student strengths, and is differentiated and personalized.
- Promote the effective use of technology in the service of teaching and learning.
- Employ valid assessments that are consistent with knowledge of child learning and development and technical standards of measurement.
- Use assessment data appropriately and within technical limitations to monitor student progress and improve instruction.

Elements 1 and 2 of PSEL 4 include the importance of the roles of effective leaders pertinent to curriculum, instruction, and assessment. The foundations of teaching and learning (included in the transformational process of the social-systems model) are curriculum, instruction, and assessment. It is frequently said to aspiring leadership candidates that the curriculum is what is taught and that curriculum is driven by state and local policies. Schmoker[6] emphasized in *Focus* that teachers must know the curriculum. School leaders play a role in ensuring that the curriculum is implemented in a coherent system and aligned with instruction and assessment.

As early as 1922, Burton noted that there were tasks that supervisors (principals included) could assist teachers with; the tasks are:

- the improvement of the teaching act,
- the improvement of teachers in service,
- the selection and organization of subject matter,
- testing and measuring, and
- the rating of teachers.

Interestingly, Burton's[7] tasks are not far removed from what is required of effective leaders listed in the elements of Standard 4 of PSEL. The teaching act, selection, and organization of subject matter, and testing and measuring are tenets from Burton that are closely aligned to the Elements 1, 2, 3, and 7 of PSEL Standard 4. The roles of the leaders and teachers in assisting teachers with curriculum and instruction have received heightened attention, in part because of the findings of research suggesting that teachers and school leaders can impact student achievement significantly.

The Southern Educational Regional Board suggests that leaders can impact as much as 20 percent of student achievement. More recent research findings suggest that leaders can impact as much as 25 percent of the achievement in schools. Implementing elements noted in Standard 4 of PSEL is critical for facilitating instructional assistance for teachers.

Burton's concepts are also pertinent for helping teachers. There is some evidence to suggest that when a student has experienced an ineffective teacher for two consecutive years, this is a barrier that the student will more than likely not overcome.

Olivia and Pawlas[8] noted the importance of effective supervisors (who can be principals/instructional leaders) and effective teachers to student learning. The importance of the principal and teacher is noted over and over in the literature. Glen and colleagues[9] suggested that "improved classroom instruction is the prime factors to improve student achievement gains."

Schmoker[10] stated that a "viable curriculum matters immensely." In addition, Marzano[11] pointed out that the "single largest factor that determines how many students in a school will learn" is the curriculum. The teachers deliver the curriculum, which is referred to by Schmoker[12] as the "What We Teach," and curriculum has to be the focus.

Oliva and Pawlas[13] discuss key roles related directly to instruction on how principals can assist teachers. Those roles are embedded in elements of both Standards 4 and 5 of PSEL. The following are the roles noted by Oliva and Pawlas.[14]

- helping teachers plan for instruction;
- helping teachers present instruction;
- helping teachers with classroom management;
- helping teachers evaluate instruction;
- helping teachers plan and implement curricula;
- helping teachers evaluate curricula;
- helping teachers through in-service programs;
- helping teachers on a one-on-one basis;
- helping teachers work together; and
- helping teachers evaluate their own performances.

Helping teachers plan for instruction, presenting instruction, planning, and implementing curricula is essential for these elements of PSEL 4 and 5:
The relevant PSEL Standard 4 Elements for this discussion are as follows:

- Implement coherent systems of curriculum, instruction, and assessment that promote the mission, vision, and core values of the school, embody high expectations for student learning, align with academic standards, and are culturally responsive (Element 1, PSEL 4).
- Align and focus systems of curriculum, instruction, and assessment within and across grade levels to promote student academic success, love of learning, the identities and habits of learners, and healthy sense of self (Element 2, PSEL 4).
- Promote instructional practice that is consistent with knowledge of child learning and development, effective pedagogy, and the needs of each student (Element 3, PSEL 4).
- Ensure instructional practice that is intellectually challenging, authentic to student experiences, recognizes student strengths, and is differentiated and personalized (Element 4, PSEL 4).
- Promote the effective use of technology in the service of teaching and learning (Element 5, PSEL 4).

The relevant Standard 5 PSEL Elements for this discussion are as follows:

- Build and maintain a safe, caring, and healthy school environment that meets that the academic, social, emotional, and physical needs of each student (Element 1, PSEL 5).
- Provide coherent systems of academic and social supports, services, extracurricular activities, and accommodations to meet the range of learning needs of each student (Element 3, PSEL 5).
- Promote adult-student, student-peer, and school-community relationships that value and support academic learning and positive social and emotional development (Element 4, PSEL 5).

As it relates to assisting teachers with implementing coherent systems of curriculum, instruction, and assessment and aligning and focusing the systems of curriculum, instruction, and assessment (Element 1, PSEL 4), many of the constructs of curriculum systems are aligned to planning for instruction. Furthermore, as noted by Oliva and Pawlas[15] state policies often govern curriculum.

It is important for teachers to know curriculum; know what content to include; know the sequence of curriculum; balance the curriculum, that is, balance between general and specialized education, balance between academic and vocational education, balance between content aimed at immediate and long-range needs of learners, and balance between child-centered and subject-centered; and organize the curriculum.

The implementation of curriculum (the "what" we teach) is so parallel to the how we teach. The significance and importance of the use of effective teaching strategies have been noted time and time again. Amanda Ripley, the journalist who authored *the Atlantic*, noted that teaching strategies can overcome all other factors significantly. Elmore observed as well that effective instruction is about a few ordinary teaching practices that educators have known about for decades which complement Schmoker's suggestion that educators know best practices; the challenge comes with implementation.[16]

Pfeffer and Sutton[17] noted that across most professionals there are factors that impede implementation of best practices. Professionals are often cognizant of most appropriate strategies and often do not implement best practices. There is evidence that the gap exists, and knowing what to do is not enough. The following are noted by Pfeffer and Sutton[18] as reasons as to why individuals do not act:

- Talk substitutes for action:

  Talk substitute for action when: No follow-up is done; people forget that making decisions does not change anything; planning, meetings, and report writing are defined as "action" that is valuable in its own right; people believe that because they have said it and it is in the mission, it must be true; people are evaluated on how smart they sound rather than on what they do; talking a lot is mistaken for doing a lot; complex language, ideas, processes, and structures are thought to be better than simple ones; there is a belief that managers are people who talk and others do; internal status comes from talking a lot, interrupting, and being critical of others' ideas. making decisions as a substitute for action, making presentations as substitute for action, using mission statement as a substitute for action;

- When memory is a substitute for thinking;
- Precedent in Action:

  Role of precedent (trapped in their history)
  The company has such strong identity; there are pressures to be consistent with past decisions, to avoid admitting mistakes, and to show perseverance; people have strong needs for cognitive closure and avoiding ambiguity; decisions are made based on implicit, untested, and inaccurate models of behavior and performance; people carry expectations from the past about what is and isn't possible;

- Fear prevents action; and
- Measurement obstructs good judgment.

Olivia and Pawlas[19] suggest that planning for instruction by teachers is a prerequisite for implementing and evaluating instruction. There are several steps to systematic planning: taking stock of the present program; specifying the goals of instruction; specifying the objectives of instruction; designing an evaluation plan; describing and analyzing learning tasks; designing instructional procedures; implementing the instructional procedures; and implementing the evaluation plan.

As teachers take stock in the present program, there is a strong tie to Element 1 of Standard 4 of PSEL. Teachers must promote the mission, vision, and core values of the school by reviewing past curriculum, instruction, and assessment and how the academic standards align to student learning. The promotion of the mission, vision, and core is facilitated by the school leader as aligned with PSEL 1. Educators must decide if the curriculum meets the needs of the learners. This is within and across grades levels that link in Element 2 of Standard 4 of PSEL.

The learner objectives are derived as the goals of instruction are specified. The objectives include what is expected of learners. The learner objectives are a basis for the evaluation process. The evaluation process solidifies how intellectually challenging the learner objectives are and if the needs of the students are met, which are aligned with Elements 3 and 4 of PSEL Standard 4.

Much attention has been devoted to the manner in which learner objectives should be written. In addition to serving as a basis for the evaluation process, the learner objectives provide the foundations for the lessons implemented. There are varying models for what should be included in lesson plans. It is noted in the literature that Madeline Hunter's[20] model is not appropriate for all learning experiences and not well suited for gifted students. However, it is a great model for drill and practice lesson.

Hunter's model is repetitive and inappropriate for open-ended learning experiences, discovery learning, and exploratory experiences. There are three major constructs within Hunter's model: getting students set to learn, direct instruction, and checking for understanding. Getting students ready to learn requires stated objectives and anticipatory set.

Olivia and Pawlas[21] outline that a critical step to teaching is "tell students what you will tell them." Obviously, an awareness of learner goals is created for students. The objectives provide the parameters for students to know where they are going, and the anticipatory set prepares learners for instruction. The direct instruction and checking for understanding provide the teachers with a quick assessment of what the students understand.

Input modelling, checking for understanding, and guided practice are a part of the direct instruction and checking for understanding construct. In most scenarios, students need demonstration, which is the purpose of the input/modelling; to check for understanding, teachers must ask questions, observe responses and interactions, and observe specifically the body language. There is a tremendous amount of research on the kinds of questions to use.

Oliva and Pawlas[22] suggest that a great deal of low-level questions on Bloom's taxonomy should be asked. Others support the premise that a great deal of higher-order questions should be asked. It is, however, critical to meet the learners where they are. Obviously, asking higher-order questions aligns to more critical thinking, which has really been stressed as aligned to some reform initiatives.

Olivia and Pawlas[23] weigh in on the observing of body language and interactions as well. They suggest that teachers should have a "sixth sense." They should know their students so well that educators should perceive when students are confused and educators should read the body language. The other part of the "knowing the students" is for educators to have a sense of prerequisite skills that students have pertinent to specific concepts.

The guided practice provides a framework for students to determine what they know—to practice. Educators and students have concrete evidence on what the students know. Independent practice is an extension to guided practice. The difference is the students have an opportunity to practice individually and educators can assist, and the teacher then closes the lessons by trying to determine if the objectives were accomplished. It has been my experience that some teachers are not provided an opportunity for closure due to time management.

The independent practice is the foundation for teachers to employ assessments and use assessment data. Elements 6 and 7 of Standard 4 of PSEL include the role that the leader should play in facilitating the use of valid assessments that are consistent with the knowledge of learners and data analyses to monitor and support student progress and improve instruction.

These concepts also align with the necessity of leaders to facilitate the designing of an evaluation plan. A variety of qualitative and quantitative techniques may be used to determine how well students have achieved. There is a tremendous amount of resources available on helping teachers develop and implement valid assessments.

Learning tasks should occur in a sequence that best fits the coherent curriculum. In addition, the instructional practices must best fit the curriculum and be sequenced appropriately based on learner needs. Hunter has pointed out that her lesson plan framework should not be used as an observation instrument for principals; the primary purpose is to provide a model that supports effective teaching that is both an art and a science.

There are many resources for teacher evaluations. In addition, there are perspectives on how they should be conducted; how they should align with professional development; how instruction should be impacted; and so on.

The notion of teacher evaluations will be discussed in chapter 4; there is relevancy for the standards referred to as the "supports" of PSEL.

STANDARD 5: OF PSEL HAS A FOCUS ON TEACHING AND LEARNING

> **Effective educational leaders cultivate an inclusive, caring, and supportive school community that promotes the academic success and well-being of each student.**

Effective Leaders

a) Build and maintain a safe, caring, and healthy school environment that meets that the academic, social, emotional, and physical needs of each student.
b) Create and sustain a school environment in which each student is known, accepted and valued, trusted and respected, cared for, and encouraged to be an active and responsible member of the school community.
c) Provide coherent systems of academic and social supports, services, extracurricular activities, and accommodations to meet the range of learning needs of each student.
d) Promote adult-student, student-peer, and school-community relationships that value and support academic learning and positive social and emotional development.
e) Cultivate and reinforce student engagement in school and positive student conduct.
f) Infuse the school's learning environment with the cultures and languages of the school's community.

Elements 1, 3, and 4 specifically include academic needs. The previous discussion of PSEL 4 is applicable for Elements 1, 3, and 4 of Standard. Element 1 also includes social, emotional, and physical needs. According to Maslow's hierarchy of needs, social, emotional, and physical needs must be met for students and teachers prior to them meeting the maximum potential.

In Elements 2, 5, and 6 of PSEL 5, there is more of a focus on the relationship side of supporting a culture that facilitates positivism in the school's environment. The importance of relationship and the importance of positivism in the environments and cultures of schools have been noted over and over in the literature. Sigmund Freud advocated that people often replicate the dispositions and actions of individuals that they spend the most time with. The concept is applicable in negative or positive environments. The role of the leader in facilitating a positive culture and nurturing relationships has been highlighted over the years.

Phillips and Wagner[24] indicated that positive cultures are essential for positive learning. Furthermore, student and teacher success is impacted more by cultures than any other school improvement or reform initiatives. Leaders must have the skill set to assess culture, gauge steps for improvement, enlist stakeholder involvement, and implement plans of actions that are aligned with visions of schools.

In the *Relevance of Instructional Leadership*,[25] Jones wrote this about culture—Hoy and Miskel[26] suggest that culture includes the norms, shared beliefs, rituals, and assumptions of organization. An obvious goal for school leaders is for schools to develop and maintain strong cultures. Schools with strong cultures will have effective leadership with exceptional student performance. Deal (1985) identified eight attributes of effective schools with strong cultures:

1. Shared values and a consensus on "how we get things done around here."
2. The principal as a hero or heroine who embodies core values.
3. Distinctive rituals that embody widely shared beliefs.
4. Employees as situational heroes or heroines.
5. Rituals of acculturation and cultural renewal.
6. Significant rituals to celebrate and transform core values.
7. Balance between innovation and tradition and between autonomy and control.
8. Widespread participation in cultural rituals.

Selznick[27] suggested that organizations have distinctive identities; on the basis of practical experiences, Connors[28] discussed the importance of the leader in monitoring the cultures of schools and responding appropriately. She provides measures that can be used to help promote positivism in cultures of schools. Phillips and Wagner[29] emphasize that schools have unique cultures; the link is consistently made to demonstrate the impact of culture on the direct influences of both student achievement and job satisfaction of educators. In Phillips and Wagner's 2003 publication, an extensive model is provided to assess culture. Plans of action should also be established to address areas of culture needing improvement.

There are thirteen possible characteristics identified by Phillips and Wagner[30] for cultural improvement in schools: collegiality (the way adults treat each other), efficacy (the feeling of ownership or capacity to influence decisions), high expectations (excellence is acknowledged; improvement is celebrated), experimentation and entrepreneurship (new ideas abound and inventions occur), trust and confidence (participants believe in the leaders and each other), tangible support (efforts at improvement are substantive with abundant resources made available by all), appreciation and recognition improvement (people feel special and act special), humor (caring is expressed through "kidding"), shared decision making by all participants (anyone affected by a decision is involved in making and implementing the decision), protect what is important (participants keep the vision and avoid trivial tasks), traditions (celebrations), open and honest communication (information flows throughout the organization in formal and informal channels), and metaphors and stories (evidence of behavior being communicated and influenced by internal imagery).

The importance of monitoring, assessing, and improving culture was previously mentioned; however, monitoring, assessing, and improving school culture is one of the roles that school leaders must assume pertinent to school improvement. The presence or absence of collegiality and efficacy (self-determination) is an indicator of the nature of culture in schools.

Phillips and Wagner[31] define collegiality as how people treat each other; efficacy is the ability of individuals to influence decisions in their organizations. Collegiality exists when people share educational ideas in casual conversation; have access to new ideas on a regular basis in an inviting and usable form; observe each other regularly in professional roles; and coach each other. Collegiality does not exist when participants focus on blaming others; repeat familiar pain; operate in isolation; and when polarized cliques exist.

Efficacy is prevalent when staff members take ownership in improving their skills as a sense of responsibility to the community (Element 4 of PSEL 5). Other indicators of efficacy include participants feeling ownership, participants feeling that they can contribute to decisions, participants being proactive, participants solving problems, and participants using combined wisdom in creation of new approaches.

Efficacy does not exist as language use is powerlessness (I do not know), helplessness is displayed (somebody should do something), no potential solutions are feasible, and familiar pains are repetitious ("As long as I do not have to teach any other grade, I can stick it out").

Phillips and Wagner[32] note that it is important for school cultures to address children of poverty, ineffective teachers, and ineffective leaders. Constructs of Elements 2, 5, and 6 of PSEL are evident in the need for leaders for addressing poverty, ineffective teaching, and ineffective leaders. There are tons of studies linked to achievement and poverty and the potential negative impact of poverty on achievement. The Coleman Report of 1966 was previously cited in the discussion of PSEL 3.[33] It suggested that socioeconomic status is the biggest predictor of student achievement.

Brookover and colleagues replicated the Coleman Report in 1979 and noted similar findings. Other variables have been linked to achievement. Marzano[34] listed many variables that impact student achievement. However, many researchers note the significance of socioeconomic status as an indicator of student achievement. Furthermore, the socioeconomic status as an indicator of achievement is currently noted.

Kozol has also focused on the differences in funding across states and often within districts in the same state on per-pupil allocation. Detailed discussions are included in *Shame on American Schools*[35] and *Salvaged Inequalities*.[36] There are trend data to support the notion that spending per pupil is lower in areas where there is higher socioeconomic status. However, Phillips and Wagner[37] note that there is a concept of poverty of spirit.

This concept is defined as students not believing they can succeed. Another poverty noted is poverty of intimate access to adults. That is, students feel they learn to be adults by spending time with adults. When adults are absent or unable to communicate with children on an intimate level, relationship skills are lacking for children.

A third kind of poverty is the poverty of rich varied life experiences. As such experiences are absent, there is a lack of connection. And, there is a poverty of hope. This definition should be obvious because without hope, some students cannot be taught. By assessing culture, school leaders can adopt practices to address poverty. Some of the variables will be more challenging to address. Some of the variables can be addressed.

Promoting a positive work environment is extremely important; however, the importance of effective teaching cannot be negated. Oliva and Pawlas[38] note that there are three kinds of ineffective teachers: those who are ineffective and perceived as effective by peers; those who are ineffective and perceived as ineffective by peers; and those who are ineffective and perceived that they are ineffective by their peers and know that they are ineffective. Phillips and Wagner[39] also describe ineffective teachers and ineffective leaders.

Ineffective teachers often feel frustrated and overworked. They take on the following attributes: they repeat what does not work; they rely on pedagogy and curriculum while ignoring effective communication with students; they become exhausted from unnecessary efforts with highly motivated students; and they view unmotivated students as problematic.

Ineffective leaders are typically unable to facilitate the visioning process for the group. In addition, they feel along and unable to support others; they join in whining; they look for perfection; and they model scapegoating by blaming others. There are tons of resources for dealing with ineffective teaching. The strategies used will depend on the nature of the challenge and the reasoning for the ineffective teaching.

Positive school cultures are environments where visions are facilitated; there is passion; there is purpose, and there is perseverance. It was previously noted that in Elements 2, 5, and 6 of PSEL 5, there is more of a focus on the relationship side of supporting a culture that facilitates positivism in the school's environment.

Pertinent information was previously discussed linked to culture and the role of the leader in facilitating positive cultures. An important way to ensure that the environments are as productive is to promote positive behaviors of students. Positive behavior promotion is also a way to promote a safe, caring, and healthy environment (Element 1; Standard 5 of PSEL).

Behaviors of students impact the discipline in schools' classroom management. As early as 1969, the lack of discipline in public schools was noted as a problem. It has also been noted that classroom management may be the single most challenging issue for teachers. School leaders as the facilitators of positive climates have roles to play in helping to minimize discipline problems and helping teachers with classroom management. Melissa Kelly[40] (in discipline in schools) noted that the ways to improve discipline in schools are to:

- Increase parental involvement;
- Create and enforce a schoolwide discipline plan;
- Foster discipline (principal and assistant principals must foster);
- Practice effective follow-through;
- Provide alternative education opportunities;
- Build a reputation of fairness;
- Implement additional effective schoolwide policies; and
- Maintain high expectations.

It is important for the learning environment to be positive as well. The factors that impact the learning environment include teacher behaviors, teacher characteristics, student behaviors, student characteristics, curriculum, classroom step-up; time, school policies, and community characteristics.

In the discussion of the standards of PSEL referred to as the support standards 6, 7, 8, and 9, resources are provided for assisting teachers in facilitating positivism in the learning environments. Madeline Hunter's lesson planning model was noted relative to instructional processes earlier in the chapter.

Olivia ant Pawlas[41] noted that Hunter's model has been used as a teacher evaluation tool; this was not her initial intent—the initial intent was to support instruction. However, there are many tools for evaluation purposes, many of which have a focus on the learning environments. Some of these will be included in chapter 4. It is important to note that positive learning environments are the prerequisite to teaching and learning occurring.

NOTES

1. Hoy, Wayne K., and Miskel, Cecil G. *Educational Administration.*
2. Hoy, Wayne K., and Miskel, Cecil G. *Educational Administration.*
3. Hoy, Wayne K., and Miskel, Cecil G. *Educational Administration.*
4. Hoy, Wayne K., and Miskel, Cecil G. *Educational Administration.*
5. Hoy, Wayne K., and Miskel, Cecil G. *Educational Administration.*
6. Schmoker, Michael J. *Focus: Elevating the Essentials to Radically Improve Student Learning.* Alexandria, VA: ASCD, 2011. Print.
7. Burton, W. H. *Supervision and the Improvement of Teaching.* New York: D Appleton-Century, 1922. 9–10. Print.
8. Oliva, P. F., and Pawlas, G. *Supervision for Today's Schools.* 6th ed. New York: Longman, 2012. Print.
9. Glenn, W. J., Picus, L. O., Odden, A., and Aportela, A. *The Equity of School Facilities Funding: Examples from Kentucky. Education Policy Analysis,* 17(4). Retrieved September 15, 2016, from http://epaa.asu.edu/epaa/v17n14/.
10. Schmoker, Michael J. *Focus: Elevating the Essentials to Radically Improve Student Learning.* Alexandria, VA: Association for Supervision and Curriculum Development, 2011. Print.
11. Marzano, Robert J., Waters, Timothy, and McNulty, Brian A. *School Leadership That Works: From Research to Results.* Alexandria, VA: Association for Supervision and Curriculum Development, 2005. Print.
12. Schmoker, Michael J. *Focus: Elevating the Essentials to Radically Improve Student Learning.*
13. Oliva, P. F., and Pawlas, G. *Supervision for Today's Schools.*
14. Oliva, P. F., and Pawlas, G. *Supervision for Today's Schools.*
15. Oliva, P. F., and Pawlas, G. *Supervision for Today's Schools.*
16. Schmoker, Michael J. *Focus: Elevating the Essentials to Radically Improve Student Learning.*
17. Pfeffer, Jeffrey, and Sutton, Robert I. *The Knowing-Doing Gap: How Smart Companies Turn Knowledge into Action.* Boston, MA: Harvard Business School, 2000. Print.
18. Pfeffer, Jeffrey, and Sutton, Robert I. *The Knowing-Doing Gap: How Smart Companies Turn Knowledge into Action.*
19. Oliva, P. F., and Pawlas, G. *Supervision for Today's Schools.*
20. Hunter, Madeline. *The Madeline Hunter Model of Mastery Learning.* Retrieved from http://www.onetohio.org/library/Documents/Dr%20Madeline%20Hunter%20Article1.pdf.
21. Oliva, P. F., and Pawlas, G. *Supervision for Today's Schools.*
22. Oliva, P. F., and Pawlas, G. *Supervision for Today's Schools.*
23. Oliva, P. F., and Pawlas, G. *Supervision for Today's Schools.*

24. Phillips, G., and Wagner, C. *School Culture Assessment: A Manual for Assessing and Transforming School-Classroom Culture*. Canada: Mitchel Press, 2003. Print.

25. Jones, L. *The Relevance of Instructional Leadership*. San Diego, California: Cognella Publishing, 2010. Print.

26. Hoy, Wayne K., and Miskel, Cecil G. *Educational Administration*.

27. Selznick, P. *Leadership in Administration*. New York: Harper & Row, 1957. Print.

28. Connors, N. *If You Don't Feed the Teachers, They Will Eat the Students*. Nashville, TN. Incentive. 2000. Print.

29. Phillips, G., and Wagner, C. *School Culture Assessment*.

30. Phillips, G., and Wagner, C. *School Culture Assessment*.

31. Phillips, G., and Wagner, C. *School Culture Assessment*.

32. Phillips, G., and Wagner, C. *School Culture Assessment*.

33. Coleman, J. et al. *Equality of Opportunity: Coleman Report*. National Center for Educational Statistics. ED 012 275, Alexandria, VA: Association for Supervision and Curriculum Development, 2005. Print.

34. Marzano, Robert J., Waters, Timothy, and McNulty, Brian A. *School Leadership That Works*.

35. Kozol, J. *Salvaged Inequaliteis Harper Pernneial*. New York. 1991. Print.

36. Kozol, J. *The Shame of the Nation: Restoration of Apartheid Schooling in America*. New York: Three Rivers Press, 2005.

37. Phillips, G., and Wagner, C. *School Culture Assessment*.

38. Oliva, P. F., and Pawlas, G. *Supervision for Today's Schools*.

39. Phillips, G., and Wagner, C. *School Culture Assessment*.

40. Kelly, Melissa. *How to Handle Discipline Problems with Effective Classroom Management*. Retrieved from http://712educators.about.com/od/discipline/ht/class_manage.htm.

41. Oliva, P. F., and Pawlas, G. *Supervision for Today's Schools*.

Chapter 4

Professional Standards for Educational Leaders: Standards 6, 7, 8, and 9: The "Supports"

Standard 6 of PSEL has nine elements. Standard 6 is Professional Capacity of School Personnel and is described as effective leaders developing professional capacity and practice of school personnel to promote each student's academic success.

The following are the standard's elements:

- Recruit, hire, support, develop, and retain effective and caring teachers and other professional staff and form them into an educationally effective faculty.
- Plan for and manage staff turnover and succession, providing opportunities for effective induction and mentoring of new personnel.
- Develop teachers' and staff members' professional knowledge, skills, and practice through differentiated opportunities for learning and growth, guided by understanding of professional and adult learning and development.
- Foster continuous improvement of individual and collective instructional capacity to achieve outcomes envisioned for each student.
- Deliver actionable feedback about instruction and other professional practice through valid, research-anchored systems of supervision and evaluation to support the development of teachers' and staff members' knowledge, skills, and practice.
- Empower and motivate teachers and staff to the highest levels of professional practice and to continuous learning and improvement.
- Develop the capacity, opportunities, and support for teacher leadership and leadership from other members of the school community.
- Promote the personal and professional health, well-being, and work-life balance of faculty and staff.
- Tend to their own learning effectiveness through reflection, study, and improvement, maintaining a healthy work-life balance.

In Table 4.1, the PSEL Standards refereed to as the "Supports" are included. The 2008 ISLLC and 2011 ELCC Standards to which they are aligned are also included in Table 4.1.

Table 4.1. PSEL Standards

	ISLLC 2008	ELCC 2011
Standard 6: Professional Capacity of School Personnel Effective educational leaders develop the professional capacity and practice of school personnel to promote each student's academic success and well-being. **Standard 7: Professional Community for Educators** Effective educational leaders foster a professional community of teachers and other professional staff to promote each student's academic success and well-being.	**Standard 2: The Culture of Teaching and Learning** Advocating, nurturing, and sustaining a school culture and instructional program conducive to student learning and professional growth.	**Standard 2** Candidates who complete the program are educational leaders who have the knowledge and ability to promote the success of all students by promoting a positive school culture, providing an effective **instructional program**, applying best practice to student learning, and designing comprehensive professional growth plans for staff.
Standard 8: Meaningful Engagement of Family and Community Effective educational leaders engage families and the community in meaningful, reciprocal, and mutually beneficial ways to promote each student's academic success and well-being.	**Standard 4: Relations with the Broader Community to Foster Learning** Collaborating with families and community members, responding to diverse community interests and needs, and mobilizing community resources.	**Standard 4** Candidates who complete the program are educational leaders who have the knowledge and ability to promote the success of all students by collaborating **with families and other community members**, responding to diverse community interests and needs, and mobilizing community resources.
Standard 9: Operation and Management: Effective educational leaders manage school operations and resources to promote each student's academic success and well-being	**Standard 3: Management of Learning** Ensuring management of the organizations, operations, and resources for a safe, efficient, and effective learning environment	**Standard 3** Candidates who complete the program are educational leaders who have the knowledge and ability to promote the success of all students by managing **the organization, operations**, and resources in a way that promotes a safe, efficient, and effective learning environment.

The first two standard elements of PSEL 6 relate to the necessity of leaders to staff schools, whereas the following seven elements are relative to providing instructional leadership for teachers once they are in the schools. There are various authors who have suggested techniques for recruiting, hiring, supporting, developing, and retaining effective and caring teachers and other professionals in addition to planning and managing for turnover. Rebore[1] and Casterre[2] and Young are among the authors.

Prior to recruiting and selecting, leaders must be cognizant of the faculty and staffing needs. Retention of faculty and staff and student enrollment are two critical variables in determining the needs on the basis of my practical experiences. Rebore[3] suggests that there are four critical aspects of assessing need: the completion of human resource inventories (skill match of employees with needs); enrollment projections; objectives of school districts; and the development of a human resource forecast based on inventories, enrollments, and district objectives. Of course, there are often state and federal mandates that impact the number and qualifications of individuals employed.

As it relates to student enrollments, there are several factors that impact enrollments and several methods to predict enrollments. One of the more popular ways to predict enrollment as noted by Rebore[4] is based on retention percentages and is known as the cohort survival technique. Both birth rates and the historical retention of students are used in this method. Rick Newberry discusses enrollment in a blog on enrollment catalyst from the perspective of factors impacting growth.

Newberry[5] suggests that leadership in schools, quality of school experiences for students as perceived by parents, the interactions of the faculty and staff with students and their parents, parent satisfaction, reputation as perceived by stakeholders, demographics and location of school, and the marketing strategies used at the schools (like how well the school is promoted) all impact enrollment.

The enrollment in turn impacts the number of faculty and staff needed. In some instances, it is important to retain faculty and staff. Individuals who perform all of their jobs duties well, exhibit appropriate dispositions, fit the climate and culture, and meet the needs of students are the individuals most suitable for the work environments/schools.

Connors[6] noted on the basis of personal experiences that school leaders play a critical role in assessing the quality and contributing to the quality of faculty and staff in schools. She suggests that the quality of employees is directly correlated with the quality of the experiences and work environment provided for them. Her approach is very practical as she describes barriers school leaders experience. One such barrier is "climate controllers." There are four kinds of "climate controllers."

The first type of "climate controller" is the climate busters. These individuals seek out to disrupt positive things in schools; they look for all negative factors to highlight. The second type is the climate manipulators who go a step further than the busters by exaggerating the severity of elements. Manipulators will exploit individuals in the work environment just to promote negativity. The "climate cruisers" are the third categorization of climate controllers.

Cruisers are not as negative but can be as problematic. They like the status quo—will park in the same places, use the same material, and are often resistant to change. The major challenge with cruisers to schools is noted in Collin's[7] perspective for businesses. Collins says that the enemy of great is good. Collins notes that greatness is a dynamic process—it is not an end. Educators must establish moving targets particularly as it relates to student achievement. It is a huge problem as any educational processes become stagnant.

The fourth category of climate controller is the "climate improvers." It is advantageous for school children and leaders to have improvers in schools. These individuals are the most positive, most open to change, and often the most innovative. It should be the goal of the leader to retain the improvers as they can impact the environments of schools in the most positive ways. *Improvers tend* to have the highest level of professional practice. There are specific skills noted in Elements 6, 7, 8, and 9 of PSEL 6. School leaders must collaborate with staff to implement those skills; however, it is critical to facilitate in the improvers.

To retain the desired faculty and staff, leaders need to empower and motivate faculty and staff to the highest level of professional practice; leaders must develop the capacity, opportunities, and support for teacher leadership and leadership from members of the community; the personal and professional health, well-being, and work-life balance of faculty should be promoted; and opportunities must be provided for faculty and staff to tend to their own learning and effectiveness through reflection, study, and improvement, maintaining a healthy work–like balance (PSEL 6: Standard Elements 6, 7, 8, and 9).

In chapter 3, a structural systems perspective is presented. The previous discussion of the structural system focused on teaching and learning (the transformational process). However, inputs and outputs are critical elements of the model. Students were listed as inputs; faculty and staff are also inputs. The success and/or lack of success of teaching and learning (transformational process) to a large extent depends on the teachers and students. This is why it is critical to have teachers and additional professional staff with the previously described attributes of improvers. Collins[8] calls it having the "right people on the bus."

"Keeping the right people on the bus" requires leaders to gauge the climate and culture continuously and to simplify and clarify what is essential in schools.[9] Schmoker[10] suggests that simplicity is a taskmaster, and that initiatives are "doomed" from the start without simplicity. Pfeffer and Sutton[11] also noted simple, well-known strategies drive improvement in any organization. Furthermore, Allan Odden[12] pinpoints that educators know what best practices are; the challenge is with implementation.

Schmoker[13] emphasizes that there is power in simplicity. Collins also stresses that educators should clarify or reinforce priorities while focusing on the most important concepts. Pfeffer and Sutton[14] stress that simplicity, clarity, and priorities are closely linked. There is then a need for repetition of priorities that are constantly clarified and simplified. The priorities could be overlooked without frequent clarity and simplifying. The challenge with complexity is that it is a barrier to turning knowledge into action.

Leaders must create/facilitate conditions for teachers to implement best practices. It has been cited and noted several times the importance of teachers as linked to academic success of teachers. Smoker[15] pinpointed that what a student learns depends on what teacher the student has.

As noted in Elements 6, 7, 8, and 9, the leader has to facilitate practices and opportunities for faculty and staff to engage in professional practice and improve. Finding a manner to address the implementation challenges is critical. The factors suggested by Pfeffer and Sutton[16] that impede the ability of individuals to implement strategies that are known to be effective are discussed in reference to PSEL Standard 5.

The facilitative skills noted in Elements 6, 7, 8, and 9 of PSEL 6 align with the facilitative skills essential for leaders to carry out Elements 3, 4, and 5 of PSEL 6. These elements are more instructional but connect to the culture and climate that should be facilitated. Providing the learning opportunities, fostering continuous improvement for instructional capacity, and delivering action feedback (Elements 3, 4, and 5) for teachers begin with walk-through and formal observations in classrooms.

Zepeda[17] has a model in which she links classroom observations to professional development. In conducting classroom observations, school leaders assume the role of the instructional leadership. The professional development should obviously provide the framework for continuous improvement and lead to improved academic performances for students. The following (figure 4.1) is the cyclic model of Zepeda.

The cycle begins with clinical supervision that entails a classroom observation accompanied with a pre-observation conference and post-observation conference. School leaders generally conduct informal observations and/or pop-ins that lead to the formal classroom observations.

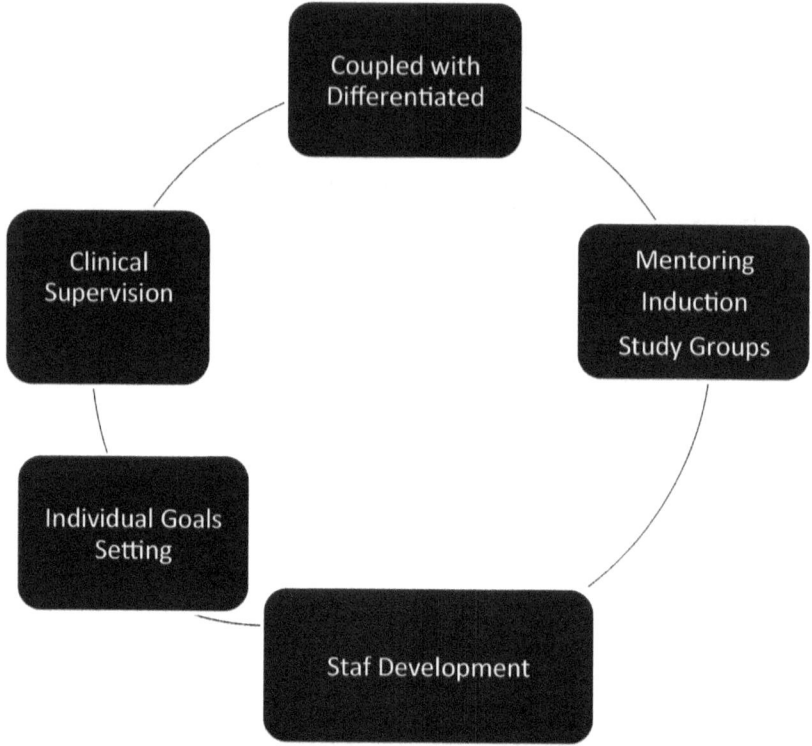

Figure 4.1. Zepeda's Cyclic Model. *Source*: Jones, Leslie, ed. *The Relevance of Instructional Leadership*. 1st ed. San Diego, CA: Cognella, 2010. Print.

During the post-observation conference, this is an important time for the school leader to provide constructive feedback. Zepeda[18] identifies characteristics of effective feedback from leaders to teachers. This concept aligns with Element 5 of PSEL 7.

The following are the characteristics of effective feedback that leaders should provide.

- Supports the teacher in examining both the positive and the not-so-positive aspects of practice.
- Promotes footholds for follow-up.
- Nurtures a sense of worth and positive self-esteem.
- Facilitates self-assessment and self-discovery.
- Focuses on a few key areas.
- Describes accurately what was observed.
- Is authentic and free of meaningless or patronizing platitudes.
- Clarifies and expands ideas for both the teacher and the observer.
- Deals with the concrete examples observed (actions, behaviors, words of the teacher or students).

- Promotes goal setting and the development of strategies.
- Guides the teacher to think beyond the lesson observed.
- Accepts and incorporates the points the teacher makes as part of the feedback process.
- Avoids
    o Making assumptions about teachers;
    o Overloading the teacher with detail after detail after detail;
    o Evaluating the teacher's overall credibility as a teacher;
    o Asserting or making inferences about the teacher; and
    o Judging and labeling a practice as good or bad.

Zepeda's model suggests that clinical supervision should be coupled with differentiated supervision. The value of differentiated supervision is teachers are provided opportunities to individualize feedback processes from the school leader and provide evidence of professional growth. After both models of supervision, school leaders and teachers can make a decision about opportunities for mentoring, staff development, and goal setting.

Professional learning communities and mentoring may serve as kinds of professional development. There are obviously other kinds of professional and staff development. The needs of the staff should dictate the kind of professional and/or staff development for engagement. The professional development must align and also lead to individual goal setting—all of which involve the school leader as an evaluator of teaching facilitates. The cycle begins again with the next observation.

There are great emphases placed on the value of mentoring. Some teachers are mentored through professional learning communities. Mentoring and professional learning communities work when they are sustained, school-based, and embedded in the daily work of teachers. Experiences in school leadership suggest that the following concepts are critical for meaningful professional development: time and organization, relevance, and follow-up.

There are many tools available for school leaders for both formal and informal observations. A reference list is as follows.

Resources for School Leaders on Teacher Evaluation Instruments:

- http://www.educationworld.com/a_admin/admin/admin400_d.shtml
- http://usny.nysed.gov/rttt/teachers-leaders/practicerubrics/Docs/SilverStrongTeacherRubric.pdf
- http://www.iobservation.com/
- http://www.doe.in.gov/sites/default/files/turnaround-principles/classroom-walkthrough-development-samples.pdf
- http://usny.nysed.gov/rttt/teachers-leaders/practicerubrics/Docs/SilverStrongObservationRubric.pdf
- http://www.42regular.com/obs/help/documents.pdf

- http://www.ascd.org/publications/educational-leadership/dec10/vol68/num04/Evaluations-That-Help-Teachers-Learn.aspx
- http://www.ncpublicschools.org/docs/effectiveness-model/ncees/instruments/teach-eval-manual.pdf
- http://www1.umn.edu/ohr/teachlearn/resources/peer/instruments/index.html
- http://www.iobservation.com/iObservation/classroom-observation/

Informal observations can be as powerful as formal observations; two sample observations are as follows (figures 4.2 and 4.3).

PSEL Standard 7: Professional Community for Teachers and Standard

PSEL Standard 7 is another "support" standard, and it has eight elements.

SAMPLE INFORMAL OBSERVATION FORM

INFORMAL OBSERVATION CHECKLIST

Teacher: **Grade:**

Date: **Time:**

YES	NO	N/A	
			1. The lesson plans show evidence of the IPS Curriculum and Instructional Framework.
			2. Evidence of differentiation of instruction is present.
			3. Students work and collaborate in pairs or groups.
			4. When asked, students can tell the purpose of what they are doing.
			5. Hands-on materials, manipulatives used.
			6. Evidence of higher level questioning is present.
			7. All students are actively involved in the lesson.
			8. Student work is displayed, current, and linked to IPS Curriculum and Instructional Framework.
			9. Students are not typically completing worksheets.
			10. Evidence of assessment/feedback is present.
			11. Classroom is organized for instruction and is free of clutter.
			12. Overall, the classroom climate is positive.

Observer's Comments:

Observer's Signature _____

Figure 4.2. Sample Informal Observation Form. *Source*: Jones, Leslie, and Kennedy, Eugene. *A Guide to Data-Driven Leadership in Modern Schools*. Charlotte, NC: Information Age, 2015. Print.

SAMPLE INFORMAL OBSERVATION FORM (ZEPEDA—2003)

Teacher _____
Date _____ Time _____ Class period _____ Subject _____
Number of students present _____

Students were:

- o Working in small, cooperative groups
- o Making a presentation
- o Taking a test
- o Working independently at their desks
- o Viewing a film
- o Other _____

Teacher was:

- o Lecturing
- o Facilitating a question and answer sequence
- o Working independently with students
- o Demonstrating a concept
- o Introducing a new concept
- o Reviewing for a test
- o Coming to closure
- o Other _____

Comment Section

Figure 4.3. Sample Informal Observation Form (Zepeda, 2003). *Source*: Zepeda, Sally J. *Instructional Supervision: Applying Tools and Concepts.* Larchmont, NY: Eye on Education, 2003. Print.

STANDARD 7: PROFESSIONAL COMMUNITY FOR TEACHERS AND STAFF

> Effective educational leaders foster a professional community of teachers and other professional staff to promote each student's academic success and well-being.

Effective Leaders

a) Develop workplace conditions for teachers and other professional staff that promote effective professional development, practice, and student learning.

b) Empower and entrust teachers and staff with collective responsibility for meeting the academic, social, emotional, and physical needs of each student, pursuant to the mission, vision, and core values of the school.

c) Establish and sustain a professional culture of engagement and commitment to shared vision, goals, and objectives pertaining to the education of the whole child; high expectations for professional work; ethical and equitable practice; trust and open communication; collaboration, collective efficacy, and continuous individual and organizational learning and improvement.
d) Promote mutual accountability among teachers and other professional staff for each student's success and the effectiveness of the school as a whole.
e) Develop and support open, productive, caring, and trusting working relationships among leaders, faculty, and staff to promote professional capacity and the improvement of practice.
f) Design and implement job-embedded and other opportunities for professional learning collaboratively with faculty and staff.
g) Provide opportunities for collaborative examination of practice, collegial feedback, and collective learning.
h) Encourage faculty-initiated improvement of programs and practices.

Elements 1, 6, 7, 8 of PSEL 7 are accomplished through the facilitation of many of the skills discussed for PSEL 6.

The job-embedded professional development opportunities noted in Standard Element 6 are embedded in Zepeda's model; the classroom evaluation process between the school leader and the teachers and staff is at the core of Zepeda's model and is fundamental to job-embedded professional development. In the *Importance of Professional Learning Communities*, Jones and colleagues (2013)[19] wrote the following as linked to job-embedded professional development:

> Professional development can be most effective when the school leader involves teachers in setting individual goals rather than dictating the parameters for teachers. Leaders must also share power and authority with teachers.[20]
>
> One example of a need to embed professional development in the daily work of teachers is that during informal conversations and class discussions with practicing teachers, many suggest that professional development in their districts is not necessarily linked to the needs of the teachers.
>
> Some district leadership have sponsored huge professional development initiatives at the beginning of the school year where all teachers across all grade levels and disciplines meet in an auditorium for an entire day with an expert on a relevant issue for the district that may not be specific enough to meet the needs of teachers at a challenged school or the individual needs of teachers.
>
> There is so much information in the literature on differentiating instructional needs for students. It is also important to differentiate the professional development needs for teachers.

Experience has taught us that the following concepts are critical for meaningful professional development: time and organization, relevance, follow-up. Many districts have the first days of school calendars designated for professional development. Although this may appear as an appropriate and logical time, most teachers are most concerned with classroom organization; the classes that they will be teaching; etc. Therefore, the focus on the professional development becomes rather limited. Timing is so critical.

There are other instances when professional development is scheduled at the end of the work day when teachers have been frustrated by the complexity of challenges of the day. The most effective time for professional development is during working hours particularly when teachers are energetic and can work.

Effective professional development planning should allow time during the instructional day for teachers to discuss the critical components of lesson planning; what is working and what is not working; and pertinent issues linked to the needs of the students.

Previously, we cited and discussed the need for the shift to occur in the thinking of educators with a focus on learning. As educators focus on the learning of students, it is fundamental for educators to observe assessment data.

Professional learning communities during the school day is an excellent opportunity for educators to analyse and re-direct instruction based on the findings of data. There is an important component of data analyses for focusing on individual students, and there is a component for focusing on whole class performances.

Revisiting the concept of professional development at the beginning of the school year—relevance is always such a critical variable. When all the teachers and other professional staff gather at one location, it is very difficult to have the individuals focus on what is relevant for the school year. Teachers are most distracted by re-acquainting with colleagues after the summer break. We have experienced many district-wide initiatives like the adopting of reading programs, special education programs, and computer-based programs.

However, it is difficult for a district-wide training to be facilitated that is relevant for all teachers across disciplines and/or grade levels. There is typically a great need for specificity for schools and teachers.

To ensure effectiveness with implementation of professional development, it is so vital to have follow-up. The most practical kind of follow-up is for professionals in the building or at minimum within the district to be able to answer pertinent questions for teachers. It does not matter how effectively professional development is facilitated; teachers will have questions as implementation is occurring. And, it is necessary for teachers to be able to obtain feedback quickly.

The research findings of Fullan[21] support the dis-connectivity of the work of teachers with their professional development. He suggests that only ten to twenty percent of teachers experience meaningful professional development. Furthermore, ninety percent of teachers have participated in short term conferences or workshops. Engaging teachers in meaningful discussions linked to practices based on the pertinent student populations is a challenge for professional learning communities.

Schlager & Fusco[22] made similar assertions regarding school based professional development. They suggest that misaligned pedagogical content can be a challenge when teachers are unable to connect the professional development with teacher practices.

It is so important for planning to accompany professional development so that there are not gaps and redundancies in training. We note that the school leader as an instructional leader plays a critical role in ensuring that the professional development is aligned with teacher practices; is meaningful and organized; and that the relevant follow-up occurs.

As leaders facilitate professional learning communities well, this provides the opportunities for faculty to collaborate and examine practice, feedback, and learning (Standard Element 7: PSEL 7) as well as to initiate improvement of programs and practices (Standard Element 8: PSEL 7). The Annenberg Institute[23] suggests that the following are the key benefits of professional learning communities:

- Building productive relationships that are required to collaborate, partner, reflect, and act to carry out school-improvement programs;
- Engaging educators at all levels in collective, consistent, and context-specific learning;
- Addressing inequities in teaching and learning opportunities by supporting teachers who work with students requiring the most assistance; and
- Promoting efforts to improve results in terms of schools and system culture, teacher practice, and learning.

As noted by the Annenberg Institute,[24] a positive culture will also be facilitated by professional learning communities. As effective professional development is fostered, teachers will exhibit efficacy and collegiality. There are so many benefits of schools with positive cultures. The leaders in schools with strong cultures have the following ten attributes as suggested by Smith and Andrews.[25]

- Places priority of curriculum and instruction issues;
- Is dedicated to the goals of the school and school district;
- Is able to rally and mobilize resources to accomplish the goals of the district and school;
- Creates a climate of high expectations in the school, characterized by a tone of respect for teachers, students, parents, and the community;
- Functions as a leader with direct involvement in instructional policy;

- Continually monitors student progress toward school achievement and teacher effectiveness;
- Demonstrates commitment to academic goals, shown by the ability to develop and articulate a clear vision or long-term goals for the school;
- Effectively consults with others by involving the faculty and other groups in the school decision processes;
- Effectively and efficiently mobilizes resources such as materials, time, and support to enable the school and its personnel to most effectively meet academic goals;
- Recognizes time as a scarce resource and creates order and discipline by minimizing factors that may disrupt the learning process.

There are obviously emphases from school leaders in high positive cultures on the establishment of engagement and commitment to the vision, goals, and objectives pertinent to the education of the whole child (Element 3 of PSEL 7) where the faculty and staff trust each other and the leader with an atmosphere of openness, productivity, and caring as professional capacity for improvement of practice is promoted (Element 5 of PSEL 7).

Teachers and staff also feel empowered with the responsibility to meet the academic, social, emotional, and physical needs of students pursuant to the mission, vision, and core values of the school (Element 2, of PSEL 7).

Sergiovanni[26] suggests that as leaders exhibit appropriate dispositions, attitudes, and/or beliefs during interactions with teachers and staff, the organization can be united as compared to becoming languished. Appropriate dispositions "transcend ordinary competence for extraordinary commitment" and require that people be transformed from subordinates to people with the needs in the organizations.

Phillips and Wagner[27] note that the manner in which individuals relate to each other makes a difference in the way teaching and learning occur in schools. Bryk and Schnedier[28] note that positive, trusting relationship among teachers and principals is critical to improving the quality of instruction, measuring student performances and reshaping governance. School leaders must be the "keepers" of the vision for the entire school.[29]

Phillips and Wagner[30] note that the vision must be understood and valued as well as modelled by the leaders in schools. This concept is emphasized in elements of Standard 1 of PSEL. As leaders "keep the vision" and build the relationships that was previously described, they provide the foundation for Element 4 of Standard 7 of PSEL. Accountability is promoted among teachers and other professional staff to ensure the success of students and the effectiveness of schools in their totality. Accountability and student performance heighten the need for leaders to be instructional leaders.

The notion of instructional leadership has been mentioned/cited several times throughout the publication. The importance of instructional leadership was also emphasized in the 2008 ISLLC Standards. The concept is embedded in several PSEL Standards: PSEL Standard 4: Curriculum, Instruction, and Assessment; Standard 6; Professional Capacity of School Personnel; Standard 7: Professional Community for Teachers and Staff; and Standard 10: School Improvement.

"Keeping the vision" as instructional leadership is facilitated is a "standards-based" role for leaders. School leaders must remain focused on what the vision means as it relates to the classroom. Elmore and colleagues[31] concluded that teachers would not automatically view the implications for the classrooms. This role of the leader as an instructional leader transcends into school improvement (PSEL 1 and 10).

In the *Relevance of Instructional Leadership*,[32] Jones noted the benefits of/to instructional leadership.

> One benefit of instructional leadership is that it provides for a collaborative learning environment where learning is not confined to the classroom and is the objective of all educators. Instructional leadership is an important departure from the ancient model of administrator as authoritarian. Inherent in the concept is the idea that learning should be a top-down process. If those in charge of the school are excited about learning, then they will share their enthusiasm throughout the community.
>
> Those who learn to be instructional leaders acquire many characteristics that are beneficial to their schools and communities. Instructional leaders exhibit a clear sense of direction for their schools and prioritize and focus attention on the things that really matter in terms of the work of students.
>
> Furthermore, instructional leaders know what is happening in their classrooms and develop the capacities of staff by building on their strengths and reducing their weaknesses. These leaders also attempt to sustain improvement and change in their schools by anticipating and overcoming the obstacles that inevitably will emerge along the way.

I previously mentioned the PSEL Standards in which instructional leadership is emphasized (4, 6, 7, and 10). The benefits of instructional leadership cited earlier relate to the PSEL in which instructional leadership skills are noted. The connection of the instructional leader to the classroom facilitates effective leaders who support and develop systems of curriculum, instruction, and assessment. (PSEL 4.)

As leaders gain a clear sense of direction providing for the collaborative learning environment, effective leaders foster a professional community of teachers and other professionals that promotes academic success (PSEL 7).

In addition, professional capacity and practice are established in the learning environment (PSEL 6). As leaders overcome obstacles, effective leaders act as agents of continuous improvement to promote the success and well-being of students.

STANDARD 8: MEANINGFUL ENGAGEMENT OF FAMILIES AND COMMUNITY

> **Effective educational leaders engage families and the community in meaningful, reciprocal, and mutually beneficial ways to promote each student's academic success and well- being.**

Effective Leaders

a) Are approachable, accessible, and welcoming to families and members of the community.
b) Create and sustain positive, collaborative, and productive relationships with families and the community for the benefit of students.
c) Engage in regular and open two-way communication with families and the community about the school, students, needs, problems, and accomplishments.
d) Maintain a presence in the community to understand its strengths and needs, develop productive relationships, and engage its resources for the school.
e) Create means for the school community to partner with families to support student learning in and out of school.
f) Understand, value, and employ the community's cultural, social, intellectual, and political resources to promote student learning and school improvement.
g) Develop and provide the school as a resource for families and the community.
h) Advocate for the school and district, and for the importance of education and student needs and priorities to families and the community.
i) Advocate publicly for the needs and priorities of students, families, and the community.
j) Build and sustain productive partnerships with public and private sectors to promote school improvement and student learning.

Many of the elements of Standard 8 of PSEL align with the Epstein's framework regarding parental and community involvement. The importance of educators having strategic measures/plans to address parental involvement is critical. There are many years of research that note student achievement is positively impacted by parental involvement.

Furthermore, the Prichard Committee for Academic Excellence[33] indicated the following occur when parents are involved:

- students gain higher grades;
- the attendance of students is better;
- student complete more homework;
- there are fewer placements of students in special education;
- the attitudes of students are more positive;
- the graduation rates are higher; and
- there is greater enrollment in postsecondary education.

The research is specific regarding benefits of children of lower incomes whose parents are involved in their education. There are also cited benefits of all parents who are involved in the education of their students; and there are benefits for the schools where there is parental involvement. When lower-income parents are involved in the education of their children, the students are 35 percent more likely to be employed; 55 percent less likely to be on welfare; and 40 percent less likely to have been arrested.

According to the Prichard Committee for Academic Excellence[34] parents who are involved in the education of their children have more confidence in the schools; parents have high teacher expectations of their children; teachers have higher opinions of parents; parents have more self-confidence; and parents are more likely to continue their own education. Schools where parents are involved tend to have improved teacher morale, higher ratings from families, more support from families, higher student achievement, and better reputations in the community.

Epstein suggests that there are six kinds of parental involvement. With each type, there are definitions, challenges, redefinitions, results for students, results for parents, and results for teachers and schools. Some of the results for students, parents, teachers, and schools noted by Epstein coincide with the benefits noted by the Prichard Committee for Academic Excellence.

Epstein and colleagues noted the importance of the role of the school leader in facilitating positive school and community involvement. The parental involvement types are parenting, communicating, volunteering, learning at home, decision making, and collaborating with the community.

The following (table 4.2) is a framework of each type with its definition, challenges, redefinitions, results for students, results for parents, and results for teachers and schools.

Table 4.2. Epstein's Parental Involvement Framework

Type of Responsibility	Definition	Challenges	Redefinitions	Results for Students	Results for Parents	Results for Teachers and Schools
Parenting	Housing, health, nutrition, clothing, safety; parenting skills for all age levels; home conditions that support children as students at all grade levels; information and activities to help schools understand children and families	Provide information to all families who want it or who need it, not only to the few who attend workshops or meetings at the school building; enable families to share information with schools about background, culture, talents, goals, and needs	"Workshop" is not only a meeting on a topic held at the school building, but also the content of that meeting to be viewed, heard, or read at convenient times and varied locations	Balance time spent on chores, homework, and other activities; regular attendance; awareness of importance of school	Self-confidence about parenting as children proceed through school; knowledge of child and adolescent development	Understanding of families' goals and concerns for children; respect for families' strengths and efforts
Communicating	*School-to-Home Communications:* Memos, notices, report cards, conferences, newsletters, phone calls, computerized messages; information on school programs, tests, and children's progress; information to choose or chance schools, courses, programs, or activities *Home-to-School Communications:* Two-way channels of communication for questions and interactions	Make all memos, notices, and other print and nonprint communications clear and understandable for all families; obtain ideas from families to improve the design and content of communications such as newsletters, report cards, and conference schedules	"Communications about school programs and student progress" are not only from school to home but also from home to school and with the community	Awareness of own progress in subjects and skills; knowledge of actions needed to maintain or improve grades; awareness of own role as a courier and communicator in partnerships	High rating of quality of the school; support for child's progress and responses to correct problems; ease of interactions and communications with school and teachers	Ability to communicate clearly; use of network of parents to communicate with all families

(Continued)

Table 4.2. (Continued)

Type of Responsibility	Definition	Challenges	Redefinitions	Results for Students	Results for Parents	Results for Teachers and Schools
Volunteering	*In Schools or Classrooms:* Assist administrators, teachers, students, or parents as aids, tutors, coaches, lectures, chaperones, and other leaders *For Schools or Classrooms:* Assist school programs and children's progress from any location at any time *As Audience:* Attend assemblies, performances, sports events, recognition and award ceremonies, celebrations, and other events	Recruit widely, provide training, and create flexible schedules for volunteers so that all families know that their time and talents are welcomed and valued	"Volunteer" means not only those who come during the school day but also those who support school goals and children's learning any way, any time	Skills that are tutored or taught by volunteers; skills in communicating with adults	Understanding of the teacher's job; self-confidence about ability to work in school and with children; enrollment in programs to improve own education	Readiness to involve all families in new ways, not only as volunteers; more individual attention to students because of help from volunteers
Learning at Home	*Information for Families On:* How to help at home with homework; required skills to pass each subject; curriculum-related decisions; other skills and talents	Design and implement interactive homework for which students take responsibility to discuss important class work and ideas with their families	"Homework" means not only work that students do along but also interactive activities that students share and discuss with others at home. "Help" at home means how families encourage and guide children, not how they "teach" school subjects	Skills, abilities, and test scores linked to class work (homework completion); view of parent as more similar to teacher, and home in sync with school; Self-confidence in ability as learned and positive attitude about school	Discussions with child about school, class work, homework, and future plans; understanding curriculum, what child is learning, and how to help each year	Respect of family time and satisfaction with family involvement and support; recognition that single-parent, dual-income, and low-income families can encourage and assist student learning

			Results for Students	Results for Parents	Results for Teachers
Decision Making	PTA/PTO memberships, participation, leadership, representation; advisory councils, school improvement teams; Title 1 councils, school-site management teams, other committees; independent school advisory groups	Include parent leaders from all racial, ethnic, socioeconomic, and other groups in the school; offer training for parent leaders to develop leadership skills; include student representatives along with parents in decision making	"Decision making" means a process of partnership to share views and take action toward shared goals for school improvement and student success, not a power struggle.	Awareness that families' views are represented in school decisions; specific benefits linked to policies enacted by parent organizations	Awareness of an input to policies that affect children's education; shared experiences and connections with other families	Awareness of families' perspectives in policies and school decisions; acceptance of equality of family representatives on school committees
Collaborating with the Community	Community contributes to schools, students, and families; business partners; agencies; cultural groups; health services; recreation; and other groups and programs	Solve problems on turf, funds, and goals; inform all families and students about community programs and services, and ensure equal opportunities for services and participation	"Community" includes not only families with children in the schools but also all who are interested in and affected by the quality of education; communities are rated not only on economic qualities but also on the strengths and talents available to support students, families, and schools	Knowledge, skills, and talents from enriched curricular and extracurricular experiences and explorations of careers; self-confidence and feeling valued by and belonging to the community	Knowledge and use of local resources to increase skills and talents or to obtain needed services for family; interactions with other families, and contributions to community	Knowledge and use of community resources for improving curriculum and instruction; strategies to enable students to learn about and contribute to the community

Element 3 of PSEL 8 notes concepts of Epstein's parental involvement: Communication. Elements 5, 6, 7, and 10 of PSEL 8 parallel with concepts of Epstein's parental involvement: Collaborating with the Community. Epstein's Parental Involvement: Decision-Making connects to Elements 8 and 9 of PSEL 8. The findings of research suggest that there are obviously different levels of school–community partnerships, but it is fundamental for leaders to nurture such partnerships for the results cited earlier for students, parents, teachers, and schools.

The importance of relationship building for leaders with teachers, other educators, and stakeholders is emphasized throughout the publication; the term *relationship* is included in Standards 2, 5, and 7. In PSEL 8, relationship building for school leaders with parents and the community members is noted. There are many leadership styles noted throughout the literature. According to Conger and Kanungo,[35] charismatic leaders tend to be more transformational; and charismatic leaders tend to have a vision and can articulate the vision, are sensitive to the environment, are sensitive to the needs of members, and take personal risks.

Elements 1, 2, and 4 of PSEL 8 have attributes aligned with concepts noted of charismatic and transformational leaders. It is noted in Element 1 that effective leaders are approachable, accessible, and welcoming to families and members of the community. As noted by Conger and Kanungo,[36] charismatic leaders are sensitive to others and will engage in conversations. For school leaders, it is important for these individuals to maintain open-door policies (where the parents and community are welcome to the school).

Furthermore, the leader should be visible in the school community in its totality. The visibility or maintaining the presence aligns with Element 4 of PSEL 8. In some of Epstein's work, she noted that many parents will be apprehensive about attending events at schools on the basis that their experiences were negative when they were students. And, one of her research findings suggests that when schools contact parents, they often report negative information. When leaders and teachers are visible and are viewed in a positive manner, this barrier is broken.

Element 2 of PSEL 8 notes that effective leaders should sustain positive, collaborative, and productive relationships with families and the community for the benefit for the students. Epstein and colleagues (2002) note the importance of leaders to create and sustain positive partnerships with parents and the community. Through partnerships, the leaders create a "family-like" school. All families are welcomed. Communities work with school leadership to establish "family-like" settings, services, and events to support the school community.

Epstein and colleagues[37] discuss that there are characteristics of successful partnerships, and that action teams are a means for leaders to ensure effective partnerships. It is pinpointed that successful partnerships have incremental progress; connect curricular and instructional reform; redefine staff development; focus on the core of caring, that is, the six parental involvement types; and focus on strengthening partnerships.

There are five steps in the creation of action teams. First, the team is created, followed by the obtaining of funds and necessary supports. Third, starting points should be identified followed by the development of a three-year outline and a one-year action plan. In addition, the planning and working continues. Effective partnerships are promoted in schools where there is a high commitment to learning; school leaders support the community involvement; there is a welcoming school climate; and the communication is two-way between the community partners and school leaders and teachers.

STANDARD 9: OPERATIONS AND MANAGEMENT

> Effective educational leaders manage school operations and resources to promote each student's academic success and well-being.

Effective Leaders

a) Institute, manage, and monitor operations and administrative systems that promote the mission and vision of the school.
b) Strategically manage staff resources, assigning and scheduling teachers and staff to roles and responsibilities that optimize their professional capacity to address each student's learning needs.
c) Seek, acquire, and manage fiscal, physical, and other resources to support curriculum, instruction, and assessment; student learning community; professional capacity and community; and family and community engagement.
d) Are responsible, ethical, and accountable stewards of the school's monetary and nonmonetary resources, engaging in effective budgeting and accounting practices.
e) Protect teachers' and other staff members' work and learning from disruption.
f) Employ technology to improve the quality and efficiency of operations and management.
g) Develop and maintain data and communication systems to deliver actionable information for classroom and school improvement.

h) Know, comply with, and help the school community understand local, state, and federal laws, rights, policies, and regulations so as to promote student success.
i) Develop and manage relationships with feeder and connecting schools for enrollment management and curricular and instructional articulation.
j) Develop and manage productive relationships with the central office and school board.
k) Develop and administer systems for fair and equitable management of conflict among students, faculty and staff, leaders, families, and community.
l) Manage governance processes and internal and external politics toward achieving the school's mission and vision.

PSEL Standard 9: Operations and Management along with PSEL Standard 10: School Improvement has more standard elements than the other standards of PSEL. In *Passing the Leadership Test*, second edition, Jones and Kennedy[38] wrote the following about operations and management for school leaders. Many of these notions align to principles in the 2015 Operation and Management Standard. The alignments will be noted in pertinent sections.

Although great emphases are placed on the role of the school leaders as instructional leaders, it is vital for the leaders to be knowledgeable of efficient management techniques and strategies.

Furthermore, many managerial decisions are critical to facilitating effective teaching and aspects of the learning environment. For instance, both knowledge and effective use of knowledge of budgeting (PSEL 9: Element 4), human resources, and other resources are advantageous to staffing schools with the pertinent teachers and other individuals in/for the most appropriate classrooms (PSEL 9: Element 2); purchasing materials and equipment; funding professional development activities; and maximizing the use of resources that are available.

Effective leaders must employ technology to improve quality and efficiency of operations and management (PSEL 9 Element 6). Both managerial and instructional leadership tasks require the use of databases and technological systems. Employing databases and other technology is important for record keeping and making data-driven decisions. In *A Guide to Data-Driven Leadership in Modern Schools,* Jones and Kennedy[39] discuss the importance of leaders creating a culture for data-driven decisions, using data in school management, and using data in instructional leadership and evaluations.

> The importance of data-driven decisions are discussed as such from *A Guide to Data-Driven Leadership in Moderns Schools*—A systems approach, as advocated by Kennedy,[40] suggests that data-driven decision making start by viewing the school as a complex, multi-layered organization with many subtleties.

Data collected at one setting may have little validity at a second setting and may be little more than the preverbal "busy" work which drains resources to no tangible benefit. A data-driven decision making plan must reflect the unique cultural context of each school, in all its aspects and idiosyncrasies.

Towards a Systems View of Data Driven Decision

Data plans are in many respects like strategic plans. A strategic plan, for many organizations, is something imposed and largely irrelevant to the actual operations and life of the organization. Strategic planning has been described as an exercise that consumes resources and has little relationship to the life of an organization. Many data plans share a similar fate. Not because they are inherently flawed, but because they fail to acknowledge that a data plan always exists.

Whether based largely on informal observations, key informants, key indicators, or structured and formal mechanisms, any school administrator will have, written or not, a process by which he/she collects data on the health and functioning of his organization.

This data will be processed and transformed into *usable knowledge*. The problem with most data plans is that they tend to have a narrow focus on test scores and classroom instruction and ignore what processes are accepted practice. We intentionally designate this as accepted practice, because most people, when given the option, act in ways they believe to be rational (acceptable).

So, if the challenge for most data plans is that they are narrow in focus and intrusive to the existing realities, what is a more reasonable approach. In our approach we expand the definition of data to be more inclusive of the types of information that are needed to run a school effectively. A simple focus on test scores, for example, is insufficient.

A comprehensive data plan includes plans for monitoring remote parts of a school campus or of buses during transportation to and from school, ensuring compliance with regard to student records, collection and analysis of student behaviour patterns, and diagnostic analysis of test scores. A comprehensive data plan does not start and end with a group of teachers reviewing test results and determining improvement strategies for prioritized areas.

Test scores do not exist in isolation. They are impacted by the ability of classroom teachers to manage the learning environment of the classroom; the ability with which parents provide educational support for their children; student norms; teacher attendance; the school's reputation in the community; and a host of other variables.

Useable knowledge is information from these many different sources that has been translated and organized in such a way that it can inform decisions. Data driven decision making requires that we have in place a comprehensive process that recognizes the interconnected nature of educational processes; collects and analyzes relevant data; and presents it in such a way that it can inform decisions. A comprehensive plan requires the following:

1. Adopt a Systems View of Educational Data.

    Distinguish between the different types of data and focus on their interrelationships. Researchers have divided data into a variety of types:
    (The following is one of the categorizations-)
    - Assessment data include: Grades & GPA, State Assessment;
    - Perceptive date include: Parent Data, Student Data, Teacher Surveys, News Article, Media Coverage, School Website, and Discipline Incident;
    - Demographic data include: Attendance, Enrollment, Ethnicity, Gender, Disability, Economic Status, Grade Level, and Work Habit; and
    - Program Data—Institution, Culture Placement.

2. Determination of the Current State of Affairs

    Understanding the types of data currently collected, how they are used is a key stage in the process of developing an effective data plan. We noted above that every school leader has a data plan, often a mixture of informal observations, counts and the like. The same can be said of every teacher. What data are considered and how it is used is a first step to being able to evaluate its adequacy. The failure of many "imported" data plans is that they are considered by the people who must use them to be inferior to the status quo.

3. Determine Areas of Need

    Identifying areas of need usually begins with a focus on outcomes, especially those that are not positive, and working back through a series of hypotheses

    Develop a plan to collect and to process and transform data into useable information. Some data will be useful for monitoring processes and others will have diagnostic utility. An important part of these analyses will involve understanding how different elements are related to one another.

4. Develop a Data Plan

    The one notion embedded more specifically and empathetically in PSEL is the attention to ethics in the management of resources (monetary and non-monetary). Both Standard 2: Element 1 and Standard 9: Element 4 pinpoint that effective leaders are stewards over the monetary and non-monetary resources in schools.

5. Develop a Plan to Transform Data into Useable Knowledge

    This stage will involve developing the human resources necessary to interpret and make sense of available data. as to why. This process will expose the "gaps" in available information (i.e., what is collected and when it is available) and help set priorities.

As previously alluded to, many of the skills and notions pertinent to management in the standards are critical to instruction. In Element 1 of PSEL 9, it is noted that the mission and vision of the school should be promoted through the management and monitoring of administrative systems. As previously discussed, implementing the vision is critical to promoting academics: teaching and learning in K–12 schools. As a matter of fact, a model provided by the Chicago Public Schools, entitled "Five Fundamentals of Success," identifies resource management as critical to instructional leadership and whole-school improvement.

The key indicators of excellence in resource management are as follows:

- The instructional leadership team effectively allocates and manages the school resources—people, time, funds, and materials—to address school priorities and students' needs (Element 2 of PSEL 9);
- The school community evaluates and plans school programs and policies based on their contributions toward reaching school goals (Element 3 of PSEL 9); and
- Teachers use other staff, classroom volunteers, and family resources at home to maximize the amount of individualized instructions students receive (Element 3 of PSEL 9).

Elements 11 and 12 of PSEL 9 include that in working toward the vision and mission, governance processes relative to the internal and external politics must be managed. The school leader must take lead and actively push for the vision in order for the credibility of the vision to remain vital. Communication and collaboration are important among all "stakeholders," and the principal is continuously the promoter and chief investigator to work through politics.

Historically, there have been three major theoretical leadership shifts. In the early 1900s, the focus of leadership theory was on the organization—scientific management. Administrators were expected to "manage" the goals of the organization. Bureaucracy, chain of command, standardization, hierarchy of control, and efficiency are the verbiage associated with this historical period. In the 1930s, leadership theory shifted its focus to a humanistic perspective—natural systems perspectives.

The goals of the organization were minimized with emphases on meeting the needs of individuals in the organization. Key concepts associated with the natural systems perspectives include survival, needs, individual social structures, informal norms, and empowerment.

The current shift in leadership theory focuses on balancing the needs of the organization while simultaneously meeting the needs of employees—open systems perspective. Key concepts associated with open systems include interdependence of the organization and its environment, integration of organizational goals and human needs, and integration of rational and natural features.

It is essential for leaders to be conscientious and to address the needs of the organization and the needs of individuals in the organizations. There are times when the needs of the organization conflict with the needs of individuals, and there are times when conflicts arise among/between individuals in the organization. An effective leader has to develop and administer systems for fair and equitable management of conflict among students, faculty and staff, leaders, families, and the community (Element 11: PSEL 9).

To an extent, conflict is inevitable; however, it can be a source of changes that are positive. There are some leaders who embrace the notion to create a crisis to bring about change. According to Hoy and Miskel (2013), there are five models of conflict resolutions that can all be effective in different scenarios: competing, collaborating, compromising, avoiding, and accommodating. The following are the circumstances under which each model can be applied.

Competing

- When quick, decisive action is essential, for example, emergencies.
- When critical issues require unpopular action, for example, cost cutting.
- When issues are vital to the welfare of the organization.
- Against individuals who take unfair advantages of others.

Collaborating

- When both sets of concerns are so important that only an integrative solution is acceptable and compromise is unsatisfactory.
- When the goal is to learn.
- To integrate insights from individuals with different perspectives.
- When consensus and commitment are important.
- To break through ill-feelings that have hindered relationships.

Compromising

- When the objectives are important but not worth the potential disruption.
- When there is a "standoff."
- To gain temporary settlements to complex problems.
- To expedite action when time is important.
- When collaboration or competition fails.

Avoiding

- When the issue is trivial.
- When the costs outweigh the benefits of resolution.
- To let the situation "cool down."

- When getting more information is imperative.
- When others can solve the problem more effectively.
- When the problem is a symptom rather than a cause.

Accommodating

- When you find you have made a mistake.
- When the issues are more important to others.
- To build goodwill for more important matters.
- To minimize losses when defeat is inevitable.
- When harmony and stability are particularly important.
- To allow subordinates a chance to learn from their mistakes.

It is also noteworthy that the perceptions of individuals in the work organization regarding how equitable conflict is management and other aspects of equity can impact how faculty and staff are motivated to work. The premises of the equity theory of motivation suggest that people will work harder when they perceive they are being treated fairly and are being treated with respect and courtesy.

To ensure fair treatment of students, faculty, and other stakeholders, effective leaders must know and assist the school community in understanding local, state, and federal laws, rights, policies, and regulations to promote success of students (Element 8 of PSEL 9). Laws, rights, policies, and regulations impact governance in schools. It is noteworthy that policies, laws, and regulations govern more academic and managerial tasks for school leaders.

Some policies are broad, whereas some are very specific and cover a wide range of areas. For instance, state policies tend to govern the number of contact hours students are in schools and the nature of the content taught as well as a wide range of other issues. In some instances, the amount of time in specific content hours is governed by policies. The following is a sample of the number of policies and/or policy manual from the State of Louisiana's Department of Education: http://www.bese.louisiana.gov/documents-resources/policies-bulletins.

Each guidebook provides practitioners with detailed information on state policies, statewide programs, and access to tools that help individual educators achieve goals with their students. The intent of publishing the guidebooks is not, however, for every school or school district to adopt all of the items they contain. Rather, the guidebooks provide a variety of options for use in the school system, unique plans each school system and school should have for itself and its students.

There is no one plan for each student's life. Likewise, each teacher needs different supports, and each school has goals all its own. *Louisiana Believes* starts with the idea that those closest to students – parents, teachers, and administrators – should be trusted to determine the best path for children. The *Louisiana Guidebooks* are tools for them to use in carrying out that most important of missions.

Heightened emphases are placed on the federal law Every Student Succeeds Act. This issue will be discussed more in the concluding chapter as it relates to accountability. Other critical laws at the federal level include the civil rights laws, the Higher Education Act, the Individuals with Disabilities Act, and the Workforce Innovation and Opportunities Act. The link that includes the federal legislation is http://www2.ed.gov/policy/landing.jhtml?scr=ft.

Students have rights, parents have rights, and teachers have rights. The varying perspectives of rights can be in conflict in which the previously discussed conflict resolution techniques may be helpful for leaders in decision making. Often, as individuals are more aware of the rights of others and policies, there is more understanding of the basis for decision making. In cases where laws are in conflict, the higher law takes precedence as guided by the supremacy clause.

> **In the previous discussions of PSEL 2, 5, 7, and 8, the importance of relationships in ethics and professional norms (PSEL 2); community of care and support for students (PSEL 5); professional community for teachers and staff (PSEL 7); and meaningful engagement of families and community (PSEL 8) is noted.**

The value of relationships is also included in Elements 9 and 10 of PSEL 9: Operations and Management. Leaders must develop relationship with feeder schools for purposes of enrollment and curricular articulation, and relationships must be developed with central office staff members and school boards for the purpose of conducting the necessary business.

In Element 2 of PSEL 9, it is noted that leaders must manage resources that include assigning teachers and staff in schools. The importance of the leader in assigning staff was also noted in Standard 6 of PSEL. One of the variables that impact assignment of teachers and staff is enrollment. Feeder schools definitely impact enrollment, which indicates a need for positive relationships between feeder schools (Element 9 of PSEL 9).

An effective leader must initiate, build, facilitate, and support such relationships. A more important need for communication and relationships exists between feeder schools for scope and sequence of curricula. Educators in both environments should know the learning objectives and expectations of the other learning environment (Element 9 of PSEL 9).

The importance of collaboration and collegiality is noted several times in the publication, particularly in the discussion of PSEL 7. Collaboration and collegiality are often essential elements to promote communication, which leads to effective relationship. In relation to PSEL 7, professional learning communities were mentioned. These are great planning spheres for educators to collaborate on instructional planning and professional learning opportunities.

In addition to developing and promoting effective communication among and with teachers, effective leaders must build such relationships with central office and school boards. School board members often make key decisions relative to many issues impacting the school sites, and central office staff members are essential in implementing decisions. Decision-making processes can be assisted with open communication and relationships between all entities (Element 10 of PSEL 9).

Ubben and colleagues[41] suggest that "good principal leaders also manage, but they manage with a leadership perspective." Good management is needed to create and maintain environments in schools that are orderly (Element 5 of PSEL 9). It was noted in the 1970s and some of the more current findings on effective schools that a safe and orderly school climate is critical to schools that are effective.[42]

As early as 2000, Razik and Swanson described leadership as being in a period of dynamic change. A leader was considered exceptional when the school environments were orderly, and there were minimal to no interruptions. This is the expectation today; however, Murphy's[43] prediction is also being fulfilled as school leaders are required to know more and do more.

Graham[44] noted that accountability would be heightening. It is no longer acceptable to allow children to slide through academically weak curricula. Accountability is becoming more and more of a focus, which is why leaders must develop and maintain data and communication systems to deliver actionable information for classroom and school improvement (Element 7, PSEL 9). There was a great deal of discussion on Standards 6 and 7 regarding classroom observations. School leaders must collect and analyze the data in a fashion that leads to improvement for teachers in the classroom and ultimately student achievement.

There are many resources available to assist school leaders in providing constructive feedback to teachers, and there are many resources on the importance of effective communication. There are instances when difficult conversations must occur; there are times when individuals must be reprimanded; and, in such instances, effective leaders must know appropriate strategies for the promotion of positivism in the climates and promotion of the vision, while simultaneously balancing goals of work organization and individuals in the organization.

Collins[45] notes in *Good to Great* that it is essential to have the appropriate individuals in work organizations, and that individuals must work toward goals and continuously strive to attain greater goals. In K–12 schools, goal setting is critical and is a part of school improvement processes. Concepts regarding school improvement are addressed in PSEL Standard 10.

NOTES

1. Rebore, Ronald. *Human Resources Administration in Education*. Upper Saddle River, New Jersey. Pearson Publishing, 2015, Print.
2. Castetter, William B. & Young, I Phillip. *The Human Resource Function in Educational Administration*. Upper Saddle River, New Jersey, Merrill of Prentice Hall, 2000, Print.
3. Rebore, Ronald. *Human Resources Administration in Education*. Upper Saddle River, New Jersy, Pearson Publising, 2015, Print.
4. Rebore, R. *Human Resources Administration*.
5. Newberry, R. *Nine Factors that Affect School Enrollment Growth*. http://www.enrollmentcatalyst.com/2012/03/21/nine-factors-that-affect-school-enrollment-growth/.
6. Connors, N. *If You Don't Feed the Teachers, They Will Eat the Students*.
7. Collins, J. *Good to Great*. New York: HarperCollins, 2001. Print.
8. Collins, J. *Good to Great*.
9. Schmoker, Michael J. *Focus: Elevating the Essentials to Radically Improve Student Learning*.
10. Schmoker, Michael J. *Focus: Elevating the Essentials to Radically Improve Student Learning*.
11. Pfeffer, Jeffrey, and Sutton, Robert I. *The Knowing-Doing Gap*.
12. Odden, A. "We Know How to Turn Schools Around—We Just Haven't Done It. *Education Week, 29*(14), 22–23 (December 9, 2009). Print.
13. Schmoker, Michael J. *Focus: Elevating the Essentials to Radically Improve Student Learning*.
14. Pfeffer, Jeffrey, and Sutton, Robert I. *The Knowing-Doing Gap*.
15. Schmoker, Michael J. *Focus: Elevating the Essentials to Radically Improve Student Learning*.
16. Pfeffer, Jeffrey, and Sutton, Robert I. *The Knowing-Doing Gap*.
17. Zepeda, S. *Instructional Supervision: Applying Tools and Concepts*. Larchmont, NY: Eye on Education, 2012. Print.
18. Zepeda, S. *Instructional Supervision*.
19. Jones, L., Stall, G., & Yarbrough, D., (2013, May) The Importance of Professional Learning Communities For School Improvement. Creative Education 4. Retrieved May 13 2013 from http://www.script.org/journal/ce.
20. Hord, Shirley. *Professional Learning Communities: Communities of Continuous Inquiry and Improvement*. Austin, TX: Southwest Educational Developmental Laboratory, 1997.
21. Fullan, M. *Motion Leadership: The Skinny on Becoming Change Savvy*. Thousand Oaks, CA: Corwin a SAGE Company, 2009. Print.

22. Schlager, M. S. and Fusco, J. "Teacher Professional Development, Technology, and Communities of Practice: Are We Putting the Cart before the Horse?" *The Information Society*, 19, 203–20. 2003. Print.

23. Annenberg Institute. "Supporting Equity and Excellence in Urban Public Education since 1993." *Annenberg Institute for School Reform*. Annenberg Institute, 2016. Web. November 4, 2016. Retrieved From http://www.annenberginstitute.org/.

24. Annenberg Institute. "Supporting Equity and Excellence in Urban Public Education."

25. Smith, W. F., and Andrews, R. L. *Instructional Leadership: How Principals Makes a Difference*. Alexandra, VA: Association for Supervision and Curriculum Development, 1989. Print.

26. Sergiovanni, T. J. *The Principalship: A Reflective Practice Perspective*. 6th ed. Boston, MA: Allyn & Bacon 2008. Print.

27. Phillips, G., and Wagner, C. *School Culture Assessment*.

28. Bryk, Anthony and Schneider, Barbara. *Trust in Schools: A Core Resource for Improvement*. 2002.

29. Phillips, G., and Wagner, C. *School Culture Assessment*. Mitcher Press.

30. Phillips, G., and Wagner, C. *School Culture Assessment*.

31. Elmore, R. F. et al. *Restructuring in the Classroom: Teaching & Learning*. San Francisco, CA: Jossey-Bass, 1996. Print.

32. Jones, L. *A Book Review of Education in the Balance. Teachers College Record: The Voice of Scholarship in Education*. New York: 2016. Print.

33. Prichard Committee for Academic Excellence (2013). Lexiington, Kentucky: "Parental Involvement." Retrieved from http://www.prichardcommittee.org/wp-content/uploads/2012/09/2012-Parent-Involvement-KSU-Chapter.pdf.

34. Prichard Committee for Academic Excellence. "Parental Involvement."

35. Conger, J. A., and Kanungo, R. N. (Eds). *Charismatic Leadership in Organizations*. Thousand Oaks, CA: Sage Publications, 1998. Print.

36. Conger, J. A., and Kanungo, R. N. *Charismatic Leadership in Organizations*.

37. Epstein, J. et al. *School, Family, and Community Partnerships: Your Handbooks for Action*. Thousand Oaks, CA: Corwin Press, 2002. Print.

38. Jones, L., and Kennedy, E. *Passing the Leading Test*. Lanham, MD: Littlefield Publishing Group, Inc., 2012. Print.

39. Jones, L., and Kennedy, E. *A Guide to Data-Driven Leadership in Modern Schools*. Charlotte, NC: Information Age Publishing, 2015. Print.

40. Kennedy, E. *Raising Test Scores for All Students: An Administrator's Guide to Improving Standardized Test Performance*. Thousand Oaks, CA: Corwin Press, Inc., 2003. Print.

41. Ubben, G. et al. *The Principal: Creative Leadership for Excellence in Schools*. Boston, MA: Pearson, 2011. Print.

42. Freiberg, H. et al. *Turning around Five At-Risk Elementary Schools. School Effectiveness & School Improvement*, 1, 5–25, 1990. Print.

43. Murphy, J. "What's Ahead for Tomorrow's Principals." *Principals*, 13–14 (September 1998). Print.

44. Graham, P. *What America Has Expected of Its Schools over the Past Century*. PA: 1993. Print.

45. Collins, J. *Good to Great*. New York: HarperCollins, 2001. Print.

Chapter 5

Where Do We Go from Here?

In this concluding chapter, there are two excerpts from previous publications that are most appropriate to address the question imposed in the title from the perspective of the discussions throughout the book pertinent to leadership standards and the most practical applications of the standards that lead to effective schools. The first excerpt is from *The Importance of Teacher's Effectiveness*.[1] In this excerpt, accountability is emphasized from the perspective of teachers and ends with the role of leaders.

As a nation, the United States experienced many reports and reform efforts to stress the significance of the achievement of American students beginning in the 1950s, when there was a panic as Russia appeared to have won the "Space Age" competition and it was perceived that America was lagging in mathematics and science. The United States went on to experience the Elementary and Secondary Education Act (1965), A Nation at Risk (1983), and No Child Left Behind (2001). In previous chapters of this book, discussion of our current reform movement was mentioned—Every Student Succeeds Act (2015).

> Excerpt from ***Importance of Teacher's Effectiveness***—The performance of American students and teacher accountability are highlighted in many of the recent and older publications. In Fullan's[2] book, All Systems Go, Sengne[3] cites the rapid decline in achievement of our students. Segne[4] observes that fifty years ago, our nation's students ranked at the top of the world in education while our current ranking among advanced countries is at the bottom. The graduation rates at our schools reflect the under-performance of our students.
>
> Fullan[5] states that there are high performing schools throughout the country, and at least ten years earlier, Slavin & Fashoa[6] noted that there were positive changes in student learning in schools. Murphy & Adams[7] also noted in the same era that many of the educational reform efforts have not lived up to

expectations. In addition, Segne[8] documents that we have allocated money to ineffective reform efforts and real change is still possible.

According to Segne[9] and colleagues, the pre-requisite for school change must address the needs and responsibilities of all stakeholders; and change should be a continuous, evolving process guided by empirical data.

In *Raising Test Scores for All Students*, Kennedy asserts that the nature of much reform has been too fragmented. Kennedy[10] emphasized the need for positive changes in schools through careful data analyses linked to needs assessments with a focus on promoting positivism in climates of schools. In a recent publication, Schmoker[11] states that "time" is one of the critical elements for change.

This is also noted in Senge and Colleagues[12] *The Dance of Change*. Schmoker[13] notes that it takes as many as seven years to effect positive change in schools. Educators should focus on "what is essential" and "ignore the rest." Obviously, the issues of student performance, under-performance, and reform are matters that are discussed by many researchers.

Furthermore, there are other researchers who address the legislation and implications linked to accountability and reform. The increased awareness and attention on student performances, accountability, and reform have also led to greater discourse among researchers and educators regarding the roles of teachers and principals.

Todd Whitaker[14] says that an effective teacher is an effective leader, and an effective leader is a great teacher or other student growth indicators. That is, teachers who are great have great leadership skills. Leaders who are great are effective teachers. In Louisiana, reform and accountability for teachers and principals have recently been linked with the passage of Act 54. Fifty percent of teacher evaluations are based on the learning of students measured by the value added model or other student growth measures.

In the previous excerpt accountability and its importance are noted throughout. All indicators point to the likelihood that the role of school leaders and teachers will become more intense as linked to accountability. This publication will serve as a guide as aligned to the practicalities of the PSEL (2015).

The second excerpt is a book review that is written of *Education in the Balance: Mapping the Global Dynamics of School Leadership*. The book review summarizes Wilkins's perspectives of the complexities of the roles of leaders. He notes that school leadership needs remapping; and leaders will have to "balance" many roles. Fundamentals of the "balancing act" discussed by Wilkins are noted in the PSEL. The following is the book review that provides another perspective to the question posed in the concluding chapter of this publication—*Education in the Balance: Mapping the Global Dynamics of School Leadership*.

Abstract

The title of Wilkins's 2014 publication: Education in the Balance: Mapping the Global Dynamics of School Leadership is very appropriate. A critical attribute for leaders is to "balance" many roles, responsibilities, and ownership in schools and school communities while engaging in innovative practices. The practices must be effective. The nature and expectations of and for school leadership are evolutionary. What was considered effective attributes for school leaders a decade ago is no longer considered effective.

Wilkins begins the publication addressing the argument that the landscape of school leadership needs "re-mapping." Throughout the publication, he discusses critical roles that leaders must play in the future.

Book Review

Wilkins[15] presents interesting concepts in Education in the Balance: Mapping the Global Dynamics of School Leadership regarding principles of School Leadership. Wilkins notes that innovation is needed in Leadership along with greater ownership in the work of leadership. In the introduction, he identifies that Education in Balance provides a "bridge" between several related but different fields.

The fields for which the "bridge" is provided include: educational policy; globalization that is general and international; philosophy and future purpose of schooling; leadership publications with a focus on the school effectiveness movement; comparative education; academic disciplinary writing centered around educational geography.

In the introductory chapter, the question is raised: "why does the school leadership landscape need re-mapping?" Globalization tends to impact so many aspects of schools and educational processes in their entirety. It was once noted that schools are reflections of society.

From this perspective, all of the challenges in society then become challenges for schools. The role of the school leader is being noted over and over again in the literature as critical to school improvement; school management; school culture and climate; as well as functionality of every aspects of schools.

Wilkins notes in Chapter 1 that fresh ideas are needed from leaders to shape the future. The role as it relates to decision-making is shifting. There is the potential for other entities in addition to the state and national entities to be involved with decision-making pertinent to education. Such entities may include international agencies, multinational companies, and multinational consumers.

There are three senses for Education "in the balance." Sense one: "tipping points" are being approached due to policies that are being driven at a national and international level. The second sense for Education "in the balance" is that decisions by school leaders will need to be made between striking balances between competing demands and the private sectors and schools. Finally, the third sense is defining learning experiences for school students, adult learners, and specifically educational professionals such as school leaders.

Brock's perspectives are also discussed in the introductory chapter. Wilkins notes that Brock stresses that education has domains that are formal as well as informal. Brock's challenge is also discussed. Wilkins suggests that Brock pinpoints the complexities of the educational needs of students which are often not met appropriately. Obviously, this is suggestive of a need for reformation in education.

The title of **Chapter 2** is "Places and Spaces"; and the title of **Chapter 3** is "International Perspectives." I view Chapters 2 and 3 as interrelated because chapter three spins off from Chapter 2. In Chapter 2 the local and global issues are discussed with attentional to spatiality as linked to educational policies. In addition, there are concepts pertinent to leadership that can be compared across different global contexts. In Chapter 2, it is discussed in depth that leaders will view leadership differently based on their perspectives.

It is very important for leaders to take interest in both understanding and respecting the spaces occupied by others—which is addressed in Chapter 3. I also believe learning and other experiences influence perspectives. Multiple factors then impact learning experiences which lead to many questions about educational phenomena—

- What is going on here (processes and outcomes over time)?
- How are motilities influencing this development?
- How are mooring influencing developments?
- How are power relations influencing the developments?
- How are places being changed?
- How are spaces being changed? Whose spaces?
- What networks are instrumental to this development?
- What educational opportunities or interests are being limited by these processes?
- Why? What rationales or motivations appear to be influential?

Most educators will agree that there are challenges in education which calls for action. In **Chapter 4,** Wilkins notes that a comprehensive plan includes a humanitarian approach. Sicone[16] noted that as it relates to teaching; educators know what best practices are. The challenge often comes with implementation which somewhat aligns with points in Pfeffer and Sutton's[17] The Knowing Doing Gap. This publication has a focus on all professionals not just educators. But Pfeffer and Sutton[18] note the many variables hamper professionals implementing best practices.

Disposition-centered strategies are noted in Chapter 4. Therefore, the concepts noted by Sicone[19] and Pfeffer and Sutton[20] must be applied as it relates to humanitarian dispositions. For school leaders, it is very important to provide facilitated leadership for teachers relative to teaching. It is equally important to exhibit concern for the well-being of the "whole persons." There is a quote often made: "people don't care how much you know until they know that you care." Concepts of giving, activism, and global scaled activism are among the principles stressed.

In Chapters 1 through 4; much of the discussion centers on the role of school leaders in their respective school sites and the impact on leadership from international entities. **In chapter 5,** there is a shift in the role that leaders play as it relates to impacting the educational community beyond the leader's institution. There are benefits for leaders who are involved in building relationships between schools, homes, workplaces, and civic organizations.

Epstein is a leading advocate of parental involvement. She, along with her colleagues has done a great deal of research as aligned with the role parents have in improving education. She notes that there are six kinds of parental involvement—parenting, communication, volunteering, decision-making, learning—at-home, and community involvement. With each type of parental involvement, there are challenges and redefinitions.

Many of the principles noted by Wilkins align with premises from Epstein's work. Wilkins discusses the importance of local support for schools. He discusses education as an aspect of civil society which definitely links parental involvement to schools as emphasized by Epstein. Wilkins also discusses Education as a commodity which definitely aligns with Epstein's work.

In the introductory chapter, Wilkins notes that innovation is needed for the future from school leaders. Such innovative ideas must also be put into practice. As previously cited, Wilkins specifically notes that "fresh ideas are needed." In **Chapter 6,** the importance of innovation is discussed from the perspectives of context—specificity. What is innovative in one school may not be innovative in another school. Obviously, innovation is a process; and school leaders must have the desire to engage in new manners to do business.

School leaders must develop "spaces" for operation and advocate for such spaces while school communities are led into engagement. In **Chapter 7,** the notion of developing spaces for operation and advocating while communities are engaged is discussed from the framework of the impact of orthodoxies which form exercises of power. Then, there are controversial issues that evolved as a results of such factors in which leaders must be skilful decision-makers. The "spaces" for leaders then transform from prescriptive to negotiable spaces.

Chapters 8 and 9 are married as in Chapter 8, Wilkins discusses the necessary ingredients for educational leaders to have a "stronger professional identity" whereas in Chapter 9, there is a focus on Professional Development. The investment in professional development from multiple perspectives is discussed in Chapter 9 which provides the pathway to the "stronger professional identity."

The third excerpt in this concluding chapter is from *Passing the Leadership Test*, second edition. In the first excerpt in the chapter (*The Importance of Teacher's Effectiveness*) the attention to student performances as aligned with the accountability movements is noted. The second excerpt—the book review on *Education in Balance*—highlights the importance of the role of the school leader. The role of the school leaders along with teachers will be critical as linked to accountability for the future.

The following discussion provides a rather current framework of the effective skills needed for leaders to be leaders of effective organizations. Two of the perspectives have specificity to schools; however, there are notions that we can learn from the Darden Business's School perspective. And in each of the following perspectives (table 5.1), there is a link to the practicalities of many elements of the standards in PSEL.

From Passing the Leadership—Edition 2

The first column of Table 5.1 includes the ten conditions of High Performing Schools from Blase, Blase, & Phillips.[21] The second column includes the six characteristics of High Performing Schools from Blankstein[22] *Failure Is Not an Option*. The third column is from Darden's Business School—7S' Perspective of the Leader's Guide to Understanding Complex Organizations originally developed by McKinsey.

Obviously, the focus in column three developed by McKinsey is on businesses whiles Blasé, Blasé, & Phillips[23] and Blankstien's[24] focus is on schools. Amazing, all three models target the role of the leader. Blasé, Blasé & Phillips[25] suggest that one of the characteristics of high performing schools is strong administrative leadership.

Table 5.1. Three Perspectives of Critical Variables for Success in Organizations

Handbook—Blasé, Blasé, and Phillips (2010)	*Failure Is Not an Option*—Blankstein (2010)	Darden's Business—UVA-7 S Perspective
Safe and orderly school environment	Common mission, vision, values, and goals	Strategy
Strong administrative leadership	Ensuring achievement for all students with systems for prevention and intervention	Structure
Primary focus on learning	Collaboration focused on teaching and learning	Systems
Maximizing learning time	Using data to guide decision making and continuous improvement	Superordinate goals
Monitoring student progress	Gaining active engagement from family and community	Style
Academically heterogeneous class assignments	Building sustainable leadership capacity	Staff (people)
Flexible in-class groups		Skills
Small class size		
Supportive classroom climate		
Parent and community involvement		

Blasé, Blasé, & Phillip[26] suggest that the behaviors of the leader impacts student achievement which is aligned with the important principles of Instructional Leadership. Furthermore, Maranzo, Waters & McNulty[27] suggest that there are many leadership dispositions and skills that impact student achievement. The largest variables are:

- Situational Awareness (principal's awareness of details and occurrences in school and use of information to address problems);
- Intellectual Stimulation (principal's assurance of currency of theory and practices aligned with school culture);
- Change Agent (Principal's challenging of status quo);
- Input (Principal's Involvement of teachers in important decisions);
- Culture (Principal's fostering of shared beliefs ad sense of community and);
- Monitors/Evaluates (Principal's monitoring of practices and the impact on student learning).

Blankstein's[28] six characteristic of High Performing Schools is the building of leadership Capacity. Effective leaders "build cultures of leadership." It is difficult for an effective learning organization to function dependent on a single dynamic leader. Dynamic leaders empower others to lead. Embedded in Standards 5, 6, and 10 of PSEL and ELCC Standard 2 is the important role of the leader in building leadership capacity among the teaching staff. The capacity is developed through the leader building a positive culture and empowering staff.

The 7 S Model presented in Column 3 of Table 5.1: Three Perspectives of Critical Variables for Success in Organizations was originally developed by McKinsey.[29] The Model was redesigned several times. The most recent redesign from Pascale and Athos acknowledges the role of the leader as interrelated to all other components of the model. The leader is critical to success of businesses in the model. The models of Blankstein's[30] and Blasé, Blasé, & Phillips[31] highlight the importance of leaders pertinent to Instructional Leadership.

The accountability movements linked to A Nation At Risk; NCLB; and the current reauthorization have all pinpointed the under-performance of students in K-12 schools. As previously cited, Scionne[32] suggests that the two single most important variables as linked to student achievement are teachers and principals.

For the three excerpts in this chapter, the practicalities of PSEL and the discussion throughout the book regrading PSEL are significant for what is expected of current leaders and the evolutionary nature of leadership expectations. There have been a number of shifts in what is expected of leaders, and there is the potential for more shifts. There have also been many accountability movements and legislation tied to accountability movements. The accountability movements have been discussed and/or alluded to throughout the book.

The one variable that is appearing to be a constant throughout the accountability shifts is student achievement. And, for some time, the role of teachers and leaders in improving student achievement has become more domineering parts of the discussion. The relevance of the three excerpts is hopefully obvious to address the question posed in the title of the chapter.

NOTES

1. Block, E. et al. *The Importance of Teacher's Effectiveness*. Creative Education. 3. Retrieved February 18, 2013, from http://www.ScriTP.org/journal/ce (October 2012).

2. Fullan, M. *All Systems Go: The Change Imperative for Whole System Reform*. Thousand Oaks, California: Corwin Press, 2010. Print.

3. Senge, P. et al. *The Dance of Change*. New York: Doubleday Publishers, 1999. Print.

4. Senge, P. et al. *The Dance of Change*.

5. Fullan, M. *All Systems Go: The Change Imperative for Whole System Reform*.

6. Slavin, R., and Fashola, O. S. *Show Me the Evidence: Proven and Promising Programs for American Schools*. Thousand Oaks, CA: Corwin Press, 1998. Print.

7. Murphy, J., and Adams, J. E. Jr. "Reforming America's Schools 1980–2000." *Journal of Educational Administration*, 36(5), 426–44. 1998. Print.

8. Senge, P. et al. *The Dance of Change*.

9. Senge, P. et al. *The Dance of Change*.

10. Kennedy, E. *Raising Test Scores for All Students*. Thousand Oaks, CA: Corwin Press, 2003, Print.

11. Schnoker, Michael J. *Focus: Elevating the Essentials to Radically Improve Student Learning*. Houghton Mifflin Harcourt. Orlando FL. 2003.

12. Senge, P. et al. *The Dance of Change*.

13. Schmoker, Michael J. *Focus: Elevating the Essentials to Radically Improve Student Learning*.

14. Whitaker, Todd. *What Great Teachers Do Differently: 17 Things That Matter Most*. 2nd ed. New York: Routledge Publication. 2012. Print.

15. Wilkins, R. *Education in the Balance: Mapping the Global Dynamics of School Leadership*. New York: Bloomsbury Academic, 2014. Print.

16. Siccone, F. *Essential Skills for Effective School Leadership*. Boston, MA: Pearson. 2012. Print.

17. Pfeffer, Jeffrey, and Sutton, Robert I. *The Knowing-Doing Gap*.

18. Pfeffer, Jeffrey, and Sutton, Robert I. *The Knowing Doing Gap*.

19. Siccone, F. *Essential Skills for Effective School Leadership*.

20. Siccone, F. *Essential Skills for Effective School Leadership*.

21. Blasé, J., Blasé, J., and Phillips, D. *Handbook of School Improvement: How High-Performing Principals Create High-Performing Schools*. Thousand Oaks, California: Corwin, 2010. Print.

22. Blankstein, A. *Failure Is Not an Option: 6 Principles for Making Student Success the Only Option*. Thousand Oaks, California: Corwin, 2010. Print.

23. Blasé, J, Blasé, J., and Phillips, D. *Handbook of School Improvement: How High-Performing Principals Create High-Performing Schools*.

24. Blankstein, A. *Failure Is Not an Option: 6 Principles for Making Student Success the Only Option.*

25. Blasé, J, Blasé, J., and Phillips, D. *Handbook of School Improvement: How High-Performing Principals Create High-Performing Schools.*

26. Blasé, J., Blasé, J., and Phillips, D. *Handbook of School Improvement: How High-Performing Principals Create High-Performing Schools.*

27. Marzano, Robert J. et al. *What Works in Schools: Facilitator's Guide.* Alexandria, VA: Association for Supervision and Curriculum Development, 2003. Print.

28. Blankstein, A. *Failure Is Not an Option: 6 Principles for Making Student Success the Only Option.*

29. McKinney. The Mckinsey 7 S Framework. Bloomsburry Academic. Retrieved from https://www. mindtools.com/pages/article/newsSTR_9.htm.

30. Blankstein, A. *Failure Is Not an Option: 6 Principles for Making Student Success the Only Option.*

31. Blasé, J., Blasé, J., and Phillips, D. *Handbook of School Improvement: How High-Performing Principals Create High-Performing Schools.*

32. Siccone, F. *Essential Skills for Effective School Leadership.*

About the Author

Leslie Jones is the primary author of *A Guide to Data Driven Leadership;* the first and second editions of *Passing the Leadership Test*; editor of both editions of *The Relevance of Instructional Leadership*; and contributing author to *All Children Can Learn* and *Raising Test Scores for All Students*. In addition, she has written numerous articles. Leslie Jones has contributed twenty-five years to public education in Louisiana in varied K–12 and higher education roles. Her PhD is from Louisiana State University in administration and supervision, and she is currently the dean of the College of Education at Nicholls State University in Thibodaux, Louisiana. Leslie is a member of several educational associations and is also on the editorial board for the *Journal of Creative Education*.

www.ingramcontent.com/pod-product-compliance
Lightning Source LLC
Chambersburg PA
CBHW032030230426
43671CB00005B/265